DATE DUE		

Ancient Rome
From Founding to Fall: A History of Rome

Don Nardo

**LUCENT
BOOKS®**

THOMSON

GALE

San Diego • Detroit • New York • San Francisco • Cleveland • New Haven, Conn. • Waterville, Maine • London • Munich

LIBRARY OF CONGRESS CATALOGING-IN-PUBLICATION DATA

Nardo, Don, 1947–
  From founding to fall: a history of Rome / by Don Nardo.
    p. cm. — (The lucent library of historical eras. Ancient Rome)
Summary: Explores the Roman Empire from its mythical founding by Romulus, through
development and expansion to decline after the barbarian invasions of the fourth and
fifth centuries.
Includes bibliographical references and index.
   ISBN 1-59018-254-5 (hardback : alk. paper)
  1. Rome—History—Juvenile literature. 2. Rome—History. I. Title. II. Series.
  DG209.N27 2003
  937—dc21
                                             2003000406

Contents

Foreword

Looking back from the vantage point of the present, history can be viewed as a myriad of intertwining roads paved by human events. Some paths stand out—broad highways whose mileposts, even from a distance of centuries, are clear. The events that propelled the rise to power of Germany's Third Reich, its role in World War II, and its eventual demise, for example, are well defined and documented.

Other roads are less distinct, their route sometimes hidden from view. Modern legislatures may have developed from old tribal councils, for example, but the links between them are indistinct in places, open to discussion and interpretation.

The architecture of civilization—law, religion, art, science, and government—as well as the more everyday aspects of our culture—what we eat, what we wear—all developed along the historical roads and byways. In that progression can be traced every facet of modern life.

A broad look back along these roads reveals that many paths—though of vastly different character—seem to converge at a few critical junctions. These intersections are those great historical eras that echo over the long, steady course of human history, extending beyond the past and into the present.

These epic periods of time are the focus of Lucent's Library of Historical Eras. They shine through the mists of history like beacons, illuminated by a burst of creativity that propels events forward—so bright that we, from thousands of years away, can clearly see the chain of events leading to the present.

Each Lucent Library of Historical Eras consists of a set of books that highlight various aspects of these major eras. For example, the Elizabethan England library features volumes on Queen Elizabeth I and her court, Elizabethan theater, the great playwrights, and everyday life in Elizabethan London.

The mini-library approach allows for the division of each era into its most significant and most interesting parts and the exploration of those parts in depth. Also, social and cultural trends as well as illustrative documents and eyewitness accounts can be prominently featured in individual volumes.

Lucent's Library of Historical Eras presents a wealth of information to young readers. The lively narrative, fully documented primary and secondary source quotations, maps, photographs, sidebars, and annotated bibliographies serve as launching points for class discussion and further research.

In studying the great historical eras, students also develop a better understanding of our own times. What we learn from the past and how we apply it in the present may shape the future and may determine whether our era will be a guiding light to those traveling future roads.

Introduction

What the Histories Do Not Tell

General histories of past eras invariably use a broad brush to paint a picture of how governments, armies, and important people brought about the rise and fall of nations, empires, or civilizations. This brief history of ancient Rome is no exception. Indeed, in the case of Rome, the sheer size of the subject necessitates using an exceptionally broad brush.

For one thing, ancient Roman civilization was extremely long-lived. It lasted from the eighth century B.C. to the early sixth century A.D., a span of more than twelve centuries; put another way, Rome was a distinct nation-state more than five times longer than the United States has been so far.

Moreover, during all those centuries, Rome underwent a steady political and social evolution. In the beginning it was ruled by kings; then it became a republic with elected leaders and a senate; and, finally, the Republic was replaced by the Empire, an autocratic government ruled by a succession of emperors. Along the way there were innumerable wars, conquests, rebellions, coups, assassinations, and foreign invasions. Simply describing in the briefest terms the major events and personalities involved in this long history is enough to fill a medium-sized volume.

The Powerful Versus the Powerless

What the general histories of Rome do not usually tell are the stories of minor events and personalities and the attitudes and daily realities of common Romans. This is partly because such information is often lacking in the ancient sources. The fact is that most ancient writers were members of the upper or ruling classes, and their works dealt mainly with the lives of the rich, famous, and powerful. Their references to powerless people, such as women, children, and slaves, and to Romans of average and less than average means are few, superficial, and concerned mainly with unusual or noteworthy examples and situations. "One of the problems about the literary evidence," scholar Thomas Wiedemann writes, "is that what was thought worth noting down was almost always what was exceptional."[1]

One result of this unbalanced view of Roman society is that a great deal is known about wealthy, influential, larger-than-life figures such as the military general Julius Caesar, the orator Cicero, and many of the emperors; the ancient writers expounded liberally about the battles such men fought, the enemies they bested, the laws they enacted, and the great buildings they erected. Thus, as University of Louisville scholar Robert Kebric puts it, for most people the word "Rome" "inevitably conjures up images of armies, oppression, [and] unrivaled grandeur and spectacle."[2]

Yet the Roman elites whose deeds fill most of the space in the history books represented only a tiny fraction of the population in any given time and place. More importantly, their accomplishments would have been impossible without the mothers who raised them; the servants who did all their menial work, freeing them to pursue greater things; the common soldiers who manned their armies and often died for them; and the laborers who toiled to raise their monuments. The vast majority of these helpers and supporters are nameless and faceless in the ancient chronicles. So with a few exceptions, they remain equally anonymous in modern histories of Rome. Despite their obscurity, however, through the collective effect of their contributions, they helped to shape the course of history as much as the orators, generals, and emperors.

Therefore, when one reads that Julius Caesar conquered Gaul (what is now France) in the first century B.C., one must keep in mind that he only conceived the plan and gave the orders; his soldiers did the actual work. Similarly, when a historical narrative says that Rome prospered in the first century A.D., that prosperity was the result of a collective, ongoing effort by a handful of political leaders, a few thousand high- and low-level bureaucrats, and millions of industrious merchants, traders, builders, farmers, sailors, and others.

An Intriguing but Disturbing World

Of course, political leaders, bureaucrats, merchants, and farmers exist today in all Western industrialized societies. Yet the world they inhabit and the problems they face differ significantly from the world and problems of the ancient Romans. This is another limitation of the general histories of Rome—namely, that they tend to take for granted that the reader knows how different Roman society was from modern Western society. There were similarities, to be sure. People lived in houses and apartments, walked on paved roads, ate many of the same foods, attended the theater, took part in elections, and went to the barbershop.

Yet the differences were much more fundamental and crucial. For instance, there was no electricity, so people had to use torches and oil lamps to dispel the darkness. Similarly, there were no

7

telephones, telegrams, or faxes, so messages had to be carried by hand; no radio, TV, or other mass media, so all entertainment was live and advertisements were written on public walls; and no internal combustion engines or other complex machinery, so all physical labor utilized the muscles of humans and animals, aided by some simple wheels, levers, and pulleys. Noted classical scholar Jo-Ann Shelton provides other examples:

> The majority of ancient Romans were poor, compared to us, and many lived at subsistence level. Our own society is also quite mobile. Many of us travel away from the community in which we were born; as we move, we tend to lose touch with our cultural heritage. Most people in the ancient world, however, remained in the same community as their fathers and forefathers. . . . We live in a society which is essentially classless, and it is sometimes difficult for us to understand what it means to live in a society like that of ancient Rome, with rigid class distinc-

Slaves are sold on a Roman auction block. Roman society depended on the institution of slavery.

tions and little social mobility. We are, in addition, so accustomed to excellent medical care, and to good health . . . that we may forget that in the ancient Roman world many people died very young, many lived with considerable pain, and many were hungry. These realities of ancient life [are] frequently neglected in political histories.[3]

Another major difference between ancient Roman society and its modern Western counterparts is the institution of slavery. No single people in history utilized the labor of slaves as much as the ancient Romans did. Indeed, slaves and the complex traditions and customs surrounding them pervaded and helped to shape all areas of Roman life, including the home, agriculture, trade and industry, the arts, the law courts, and the government. Moreover, Romans of all walks of life, slaves and freedmen (ex-slaves) included, accepted slavery as a normal and inevitable fact of life. (Many freedmen routinely acquired slaves of their own.) So, when one reads in a general history text that the emperor Hadrian traveled extensively throughout the Empire in the early second century, one needs to picture him accompanied by hundreds of slaves and freedmen who catered to his every whim. One must also picture a so-

ciety in which even households of moderate means had slaves; in which masters could beat, sexually abuse, and even kill slaves, usually with few or no consequences; and in which many masters lived in perpetual fear of their slaves turning on them.

As a rule, general histories lack the space to tell about these and other important realities of the lives of the ancient Romans. So modern readers of such histories must always keep in mind that the deeds and events described took place in a society they would find somewhat familiar, perhaps intriguing, but in many ways alien and disturbing. It was a society in which people's aspirations, social rights and opportunities, worldview, and even their sense of right and wrong were often very different from those common today.

Finally, no general history of Rome can convey the personal feelings of the vast majority of its long-dead inhabitants. Except for a tiny handful who expressed themselves in memoirs that have survived, the thoughts and feelings of all the rest are lost forever in the mists of time. In the words of historian L.P. Wilkinson, "We can gather what . . . Cicero felt from his letters, what the emperor Marcus Aurelius felt from his [books of] 'meditations,' [but] it is hard to discover or imagine what the ordinary, inarticulate person felt."[4]

Rome's Origins and Early Rulers

Today the exact origins of Rome are uncertain. But the ancient Romans themselves had no doubt how their so-called eternal city was born. Practically any man or woman on the Roman street could tell the traditional tale of Romulus, who founded Rome and served as its first king. According to the story, Romulus and his twin brother, Remus, belonged to the royal house of Alba Longa, a town located on the plain of Latium, south of the site where Rome would eventually rise. Their grandfather Numitor was king. But shortly after their birth, Numitor's brother, Amulius, stole the throne and ordered the babies to be drowned in the Tiber River. The men entrusted with this grisly deed put the infant boys in a basket and set it adrift, but after the men departed, the basket washed ashore. The great first-century B.C. Roman historian Livy told what happened next:

> A she-wolf, coming down from the neighboring hills to quench her thirst, heard the children crying and made her way to where they were. She offered them her teats to suck and treated them with such gentleness that Faustulus, the king's herdsman, found her licking them with her tongue. Faustulus took them to his hut and gave them to his wife Larentia to nurse.[5]

The kind shepherd couple brought the brothers up and eventually revealed to them their true identities. Romulus and Remus were reunited with their grandfather and soon afterward returned to Alba Longa, where they overthrew the usurper Amulius and restored Numitor to his throne. Then, said Livy, the young men "were suddenly seized by an urge to found a new settlement on the spot where they had been left to drown as infants." Romulus began building a walled town on the Palatine hill, while Remus did the same on the Aventine hill. Soon, however, the two got into an argument and Romulus lost his temper. "Remus," Livy continued, "by way of jeering at his brother, jumped over the half-built walls of the new settlement, whereupon Romulus killed him in a fit of rage, adding this threat, 'So perish whoever else shall overleap my battlements.'"[6] Romulus came to regret slaying his brother, and after giving him a proper burial, went on to establish the city of Rome, naming it after himself.

The later Romans not only believed this story; they even claimed to know when the events it described happened. During the first century B.C., by which time Rome had come to dominate the Mediterranean world, a number of Roman

Romulus and his brother Remus are suckled by a she-wolf, as described in the accounts of Livy and other ancient historians.

Romulus Slays Remus

In his famous history of Rome, the ancient historian Livy describes the quarrel between Romulus and his brother Remus this way:

Unhappily, the brothers' plans for the future were marred by the same source which had divided their grandfather and Amulius—jealousy and ambition. A disgraceful quarrel arose from a matter in itself trivial. As the brothers were twins and all questions of seniority were therefore precluded, they determined to ask the gods of the countryside to declare . . . which of them should govern the new town once it was founded, and give his name to it. . . . Remus, the story goes, was the first to receive a sign—six vultures [in some accounts, eagles]; and no sooner was this made known to the people than double the number of birds appeared to Romulus. The followers of each promptly saluted their masters as king. . . . Angry words ensued, followed all too soon by blows, and in the course of the fray Remus was killed. There is another story, a commoner one, according to which Remus, by way of jeering at his brother, jumped over the half-built walls of the new settlement, whereupon Romulus killed him in a fit of rage, adding the threat, 'So perish whoever else shall overleap my battlements.'

Romulus kills his brother Remus.

scholars attempted to compute the city's exact founding date. They found it difficult because in prior centuries the Romans had used several different calendars and dating systems, none of which were very accurate. Finally, one of these men, Marcus Terentius Varro, arrived at a date of 753 B.C. This became the traditional founding date accepted through most of the following twenty centuries.

Where Did the Romans Come From?

Regardless of tradition, modern scholars feel that Varro's date, along with the Romulus story itself, should not be taken at face value. Modern archaeology has shown that the city of Rome and the culture it spawned did not spring into being in a single, decisive foundation incident. Rather, evidence suggests that the early Romans inhabited the area well before the time Varro advocated; furthermore, Roman society seems to have sprung from several small villages that gradually combined into a single town. According to T.J. Cornell, a noted expert on early Rome:

> The first traces of permanent habitation on the site of Rome date back to around 1000 B.C. . . . During the earliest phases the communities [in the area of Rome] were small villages. . . . There may have been habitations on several of the hills surrounding the Forum [Rome's main square]— certainly the Palatine (which at one stage was perhaps the site of more than one village). . . . [In time] the pattern of settlement changed, as groups of villages began to coalesce [come together] and to form larger nucleated units. . . . At Rome the habitation area was extended from the Palatine to include the Capitol [i.e., the Capitoline hill] and Forum.[7]

As for where the inhabitants of these early Roman villages came from, historians have put forward two main theories. In the first, the Romans originated in central Italy as part of the so-called Apennine culture (named after the mountain range that runs from north to south through the Italian peninsula). This society, which used tools and weapons made of bronze and practiced inhumation (burial of the dead), appeared around 1800 B.C. About six hundred years later, the culture began to experience significant changes, including a transition to iron tools and weapons, population increases, and the replacement of inhumation with cremation (burning of the dead). It is possible that this change from a Bronze Age to an Iron Age society was due to cultural influences that steadily entered Italy from neighboring lands.

The second theory about the origins of the earliest Romans holds that a group of Latin-speaking tribes migrated into Italy sometime in its Bronze Age. Some may have started in central Europe and come across the Alps in succeeding waves, one every two or three generations. Others may have originated farther east, traveled westward through what is now Serbia, and crossed the Adriatic Sea into eastern Italy. Then, slowly but steadily, they moved across the peninsula until one group arrived at and settled on the Roman hills.

Founding the Master Race

In fact, the Romans themselves had a major tradition that claimed that the founder of their race had originated in the eastern Mediterranean and traveled westward to Italy. They borrowed this tradition from the Greeks. In the late 700s and early 600s B.C., Greek settlers began establishing cities in southern Italy.

Even at this early date, the Greeks were considerably more culturally advanced than the Romans; and the latter were duly impressed by their new neighbors. Of particular note to the Romans was the Greek legend of the Trojan War, immortalized by the Greek poet Homer in his great epic the *Iliad*. In the story, a group of early Greek kings lay siege to and sack the city of Troy, on the northwestern coast of Asia Minor (what is now Turkey). The heroes of that conflict, including the Greeks Achilles and Odysseus and the Trojans Hector and Aeneas, were seen as men of larger-than-life stature who ac-

complished deeds of incredible bravery and who actually saw and spoke to the gods.

Sometime in the sixth century B.C., the Romans created a link between themselves and one of the leading characters of Homer's tale. The character was Aeneas, a Trojan prince who managed to escape the burning Troy. The Romans held that Aeneas and his closest followers journeyed to Italy, where they gave rise to the direct ancestors of Romulus and Remus. The reasons for this important cultural borrowing are not hard to fathom. For one thing, the Romans felt

Calculating Rome's Birth Date

The exact manner in which the first-century B.C. Roman scholar Varro arrived at his date for Rome's founding (equivalent to 753 B.C.) is unknown. He and the other scholars working on the problem may have based their calculations partly on the length of the Monarchy as stated in existing legends. Or, as scholar T.J. Cornell points out in *The Beginnings of Rome*, they may have counted backward seven generations (one for each king) from the accepted date of the establishment of the Republic. Whatever the method employed, the founding date Varro produced was seen as the year 1 in a dating system that reckoned events "from Rome's founding" (*ab urbe condita*), abbreviated AUC. In that system, the Republic was established in about 244 or 245 AUC (509 B.C.), and Varro was born in about 648 AUC (116 B.C.). The system that uses the labels B.C. (before Christ) and A.D. (*anno Domini,* meaning "the year of the Lord") was introduced by Christian scholars almost seven centuries later. These scholars estimated that Christ had been born in the year 754 AUC and labeled it A.D. 1 in their new chronology. In their system, therefore, Rome was founded 753 years before the year 1, or 753 B.C.

the need to raise their stature and prestige among the peoples living in Italy at the time. In addition, Cornell points out:

> It is not surprising that the Romans were willing to embrace a story that flattered their pride by associating them with the legendary traditions of the Greeks, whose cultural superiority they were forced to acknowledge—albeit sometimes grudgingly. More specifically, in Greek myth Aeneas possessed qualities which the Romans liked to see in themselves, such as reverence for the gods and love of his fatherland. The Trojan legend was also useful to the Romans in that it gave them a respectable identity in the eyes of a wider world, and one that could be used to advantage in their dealings with the Greeks.[8]

Whatever the reasons for the inception of the Roman version of the Aeneas legend, over time the story was steadily embellished and at the same time imprinted indelibly onto the Roman psyche. Finally, in the form of the *Aeneid,* a long poem by the first-century B.C. Roman writer Virgil, the tale was forever enshrined as Rome's cherished national epic.

As told by Virgil, after taking part in many adventures, Aeneas landed at Cumae, on Italy's southwestern coast. There he met the Sibyl, a prophetess who informed him that he was destined to fight a war in Italy and eventually marry an Italian woman. Then, with the Sibyl's aid, Aeneas descended into the Under-

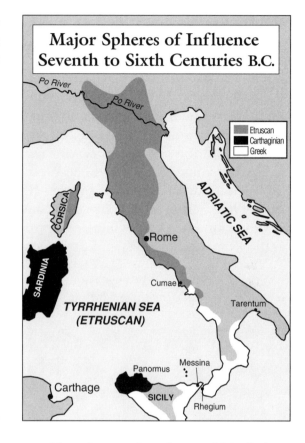

world and met the ghost of his father, Anchises, who had died during the long journey from Troy. Anchises proceeded to reveal the future of the noble race Aeneas would sire. First, Aeneas's offspring would establish the city of Alba Longa, in Latium. Eventually, Alba's royal house would produce Numitor and his grandsons, Romulus and Remus. Romulus would go on to found the city of Rome, which "shall rule the whole wide world [and] her spirit shall match the spirit of the gods. Round seven citadels [i.e., Rome's Seven Hills] shall she build her walls, in her breed of heroes blessed."[9]

15

After learning about his destiny, Aeneas returned to the earth's surface and traveled northward to Latium to fulfill it. As the Sibyl had predicted, he fought and won a war and married an Italian princess, Lavinia; and from their union sprang the royal house of Alba Longa and the long line of noble Romans whom the king of the gods, Jupiter, had chosen to rule the world. In fact, as Virgil put it, Jupiter had earlier declared, "I see no measure nor date" that will place limits on the Romans. "I grant them dominion

In this modern illustration of a scene from Virgil's Aeneid, Aeneas slays Turnus, an Italian prince who opposes the Trojans.

without end . . . the master-race, the wearers of the Toga. So it is willed!"[10]

Rome's First King

This, then, is how the Romans connected Aeneas and his exploits to their own popular local hero Romulus, supposedly Rome's first king as well as its founder. Once Romulus had buried his brother, he began laying out the city's walls, streets, and first buildings. According to the first-century A.D. Greek writer Plutarch in his biography of Romulus, the founder asked for advice and help from the Etruscans, a people who inhabited the region directly north of Rome and came to influence Roman culture in a number of ways. They showed him "the [religious] ceremonies to be observed" in the proper establishment of a city, so as not to offend the gods. Then they helped him lay down the town's outer boundaries.

> First, they dug a round trench . . . and into it solemnly threw the first-fruits of all things either good by custom or necessary by nature; lastly, every man taking a small piece of earth of the country from whence he came, they all threw [the piece] in randomly together. Making this trench . . . their center, they laid out the boundary of the city in a circle round it. Then the founder fitted to a plow a metal plowshare [blade], and, yoking together a bull and a cow, drove himself a deep line or furrow round the boundary. . . .

Romulus guides his followers to mark the boundary lines of Rome. Eventually, the new city encompassed seven hills.

With this line they laid out the [city] wall [on the Palatine hill]; and where they designed to make a gate, there they . . . left a space. . . . As for the day they began to build the city, it is universally agreed to have been the twenty-first of April, and that day the Romans annually keep holy, calling it their country's birthday. At first, they say, they sacrificed [to the gods] no living creature on this day, thinking it fit to preserve the feast of their country's birthday pure and without stain of blood.[11]

Having laid Rome's basic foundations, Romulus wasted no time in tackling a number of crucial legal and social challenges facing the new community. In Livy's account:

He summoned his subjects and gave them laws, without which the creation of a unified [people] would have been impossible. In his view, the rabble over which he ruled could be induced to respect the law only if he himself adopted certain visible signs of power . . . of which

17

Romulus's Hut Unearthed?

Archaeologists and other modern scholars have long searched for evidence that might either confirm or disprove the events of the traditional Roman foundation myth. A tantalizing clue came to light in the 1930s when the remains of some crude ancient huts were found on the Palatine hill. Excavators tentatively dated the huts to the eighth century B.C., so that both the site and time period are the same as those described in the myth in which Romulus built his first settlement. Also, archaeologists unearthed evidence suggesting that the Romans maintained one particular hut in good repair for many centuries, as if it was special or important in some way. In fact, some ancient writings mention a shrine to which Romans came to pay homage. It contained the *casa Romuli*, or "House of Romulus," a small shepherd's house preserved by the government as a relic. The Romans revered this shrine so much that the first emperor, Augustus, erected his own house nearby; presumably he hoped to increase his prestige by demonstrating close association with the city's founder. It is possible that the hut excavated in the twentieth century and the one long maintained by the ancient Romans are one and the same.

the most important was the creation of the twelve lictors [close followers who carried the fasces, symbols of royal power] to attend his person. . . . Meanwhile Rome was growing. More and more ground was coming within the circuit of its walls. . . . To help fill his big new town, [Romulus] threw open . . . a place of asylum for fugitives. Hither fled for refuge all the [outcasts] from the neighboring peoples; some free, some slaves, and all of them wanting nothing more than a fresh start. That mob was the first real addition to the city's strength, the first step to her future greatness.[12]

The Sabine Women

According to Livy and other Roman writers, another challenge King Romulus faced was the fact that the vast majority of Rome's earliest residents were men. Obviously they could not hope to establish families and further expand the population unless they could find a ready source of women to become their brides. Meeting this challenge, the king hatched a bold and stealthy plot. Several of the neighboring towns were inhabited by a

Latin people called the Sabines, whom Romulus now invited to attend a festive religious celebration in Rome. His real aim was not to build friendly relations, of course, but to steal the Sabine women. In Livy's words:

On the appointed day crowds flocked to Rome, partly, no doubt, out of sheer curiosity to see the new town. . . . All the Sabines were there . . . with their wives and children. . . . Then the great moment came; the show began, and nobody had eyes or thought for anything else. This was the Romans' opportunity. At a given signal, all the able-bodied men burst through the crowd and seized the young women. Most of the girls were the prize of whoever got hold of them first, but a few conspicuously handsome ones had been previously marked down for leading [Romans], and these were brought to their houses by special gangs. . . . By this act of violence, the fun of the

This seventeenth-century painting depicts the capture of the Sabine women, who were abducted to help populate Rome.

festival broke up in panic. The girls' unfortunate parents made good their escape, not without bitter comments on the treachery of their hosts.[13]

As might be expected, the young women were indignant over being abducted and were filled with trepidation about their safety and future. However, Romulus assured them that they would be well treated and tried to persuade them to accept their fate. As the women weighed the situation, their husbands and fathers endeavored to free them by launching an assault on Rome. Romulus and his troops managed to defeat the first several groups of attackers. But the Sabines of the city of Cures successfully surrounded Rome, and a great battle took place on the flat ground between the Palatine and Capitoline hills. Hundreds on both sides were killed before the former Sabine women rushed out and demanded a truce. They said that they could not just stand there and watch their fathers, brothers, and new husbands murder one another. Thanks to their intervention, the two sides signed a treaty and agreed to combine their populations into one people, with Romulus and the Sabine king, Titus Tatius, as joint rulers. These events marked Rome's first, but certainly not its last, conquest and absorption of a neighboring people.

The Roman Kings

Whether or not Romulus was actually Rome's first king and accomplished the deeds attributed to him in the works of Livy, Plutarch, and others is unknown. The consensus of modern scholars is that there might have been an important early ruler named Romulus; but his legend likely reflects a conflation, or fusion, of the reigns of several kings whose names have been lost.

What seems more certain is that the Roman Monarchy was well entrenched by at least the late seventh century B.C. The region the early kings controlled was fairly small, likely covering little more than a few hundred square miles. The bulk of this land consisted of sparsely inhabited farms, forests, and swamps; Rome was then and remained an agrarian, rural state punctuated here and there by relatively small urban areas.

The result was that during the period of the kings, the central town of Rome was an unimposing, crude place featuring unpaved streets that became thick with mud in the rainy season. Archaeological finds suggest that these streets were lined with huts made of timber and thatch, while a few larger structures, including temples and perhaps a small palace, were constructed mainly of wood. Except for a few traces that have survived, these highly perishable structures disappeared over the course of time as bigger, more permanent stone versions took their places. Throughout the years of the Monarchy and for long afterward, a majority of Romans did not reside in this urban center, but lived instead in small farming huts in the surrounding countryside.

The well in the foreground and the circular stone huts seen here are typical of those used by Roman farmers in rural areas.

Modern scholars are unsure about how long the Roman Monarchy existed. The number of kings and the lengths of their reigns are equally uncertain, but later tradition held that seven men ruled the city beginning in 753 B.C.—Romulus, Numa Pompilius, Tullus Hostilius, Ancus Marcius, Tarquinius Priscus, Servius Tullius, and Tarquinius Superbus (or "Tarquin the Proud"). The first three were most likely legendary. The last four may have been real people; however, it is probable that other kings whose names have not survived ruled during the same period.

Also uncertain is the manner in which the Roman kings were chosen, the exact nature of their duties, and the extent of

their authority. Livy and other later writers mention a sort of election in which some of the male citizens took part. Probably the right to vote was based on certain property qualifications, including ownership of armor and weapons, which were quite expensive at the time. So, as happened in Greece during the same period, the community's fighting men met in an assembly, a periodic meeting to consider vital political and social policies. (The Latin word for such assemblies was *comitia*.) The real power was undoubtedly in the hands of the king and to a lesser extent his advisory board, the Senate (which would later become a true legislature with much authority); but the

This drawing is based on a sculpture depicting Roman men voting. Limited to very few people in the Monarchy, this right was extended to all male citizens in the Republic.

men who met in the assembly likely ratified the choice of monarch, as well as his major policies. The late, noted scholar Michael Rostovtzeff elaborated about the early Senate and the kings it served:

> [The Senate's] members were representatives of the richest and noblest families (*gentes*). It is possible that these persons were commonly called "fathers" (*patres*), and their descendants "patricians." From a very early date the patricians enjoyed a number of privileges, among the most important being the right of acting as intermediaries between the king and the gods. . . . The patricians acted

as cavalry on [military] campaigns. . . . As a matter of course, the kings were commanders-in-chief, and also supreme as judges and priests. We do not know whether their power was hereditary or held for life. They communicated their decrees to the people at specially summoned meetings (*comitia*).[14]

Early Reforms and Conquests

Livy and other ancient historians recorded stories about specific accomplishments of the early kings. One of the most important and far-reaching of all was a major reorganization of Roman society intended to increase the efficiency of the military. It was supposedly undertaken by the sixth king, Servius Tullius, in the middle of the sixth century B.C.; so it is usually referred to as the Servian reform. This is probably not accurate, however. Evidence suggests that the changes took place a bit later and over a more extended period.

In essence, as the story goes, the king and his advisers ordered a census of free male Romans and divided them, along with the army, into six classes. The class one belonged to depended on one's wealth. Those who owned property valued at 100,000 *asses* or more (an *as* being a common unit of Roman currency) made up eighty centuries, groups of one hundred men each. "This whole group was known as the First Class," Livy stated.

> All were required to equip themselves with helmet, round shield, greaves, and breastplate. The defensive armor was of bronze. Their weapons of offense were the sword and spear. . . . The Second Class comprised those whose property was rated between 100,000 and 75,000. From these 20 centuries . . . were formed, and required to provide the same equipment as Class 1, save that the breastplate was omitted and the long [oval shield] substituted for the round shield.[15]

The third, fourth, and fifth classes were made up of soldiers carrying successively lighter arms; and the sixth class, made up of the poorest members of Roman society, did not have to serve in the army.

Servius was also famous for erecting Rome's first substantial stone defensive wall, which thereafter bore the name Servian Wall in his honor. "The population of Rome was by now so great," Livy said, "that Servius decided to extend the city boundaries. . . . The city defenses he strengthened by constructing trenches, earthworks, and a wall."[16]

There was good reason for such formidable defenses. During the years of the Monarchy, the Romans frequently came into conflict with their immediate neighbors; and the lands under Rome's control steadily grew larger. Expansion was particularly pronounced in the Latium plain south of the city. Various legends, some of which are probably exaggerated versions of real events, describe the Roman capture of Alba Longa, the hometown of Romulus and Remus. According to one of these stories, during the reign of the Roman king Tullus Hostilius (673–642 B.C.), war broke out between Rome and Alba. Both sides thought it best to keep their armies intact so that they could fight their common enemy, the Etruscans. To this end, each side selected three champions. The idea was for the six men to fight and thereby to decide the war's outcome. After a tremendous display of physical prowess witnessed by both armies, two of the three Romans were killed and the third faced

The last of the three Roman champions slays the last of the three Albans in an early confrontation between Rome and Alba Longa.

the three Albans alone. According to Livy:

> His three enemies were coming, strung out one behind the other, the foremost almost upon him. He turned and attacked him furiously. . . . [He] killed his man, and flushed with triumph, was looking for his next victim. The Romans' cheer for their young soldier was like the roar of the crowd at the race when luck turns defeat into victory.[17]

The lone Roman quickly dispatched his other two opponents, after which, said Livy, "the cheering ranks of the Roman army welcomed back their champion. . . . Alba was subject now to her Roman mistress."[18]

Though they no doubt seemed significant at the time, such conquests were comparatively minor and close to home. Rome was still a small city-state occupying only a tiny portion of the Italian peninsula. Much larger bursts of expansion would take place in the next few centuries, but this growth would be accomplished under a completely new political system. Tullus and his successor, Tarquin the Proud, had no way of knowing that the days of the Roman kings were numbered.

Founding and Expansion of the Republic

The period in which the city of Rome coalesced from several small villages and a series of kings ruled the Roman city-state was a mere prelude to the emergence of Rome as a great and influential power in the Mediterranean world. Rome's rise to greatness began in 509 B.C. with the birth of the Republic. This was a government based on the rule of the people through representatives sitting in citizen assemblies and the Senate, which dropped its advisory role and became a full-fledged legislature. Under the banners of the Republic, the Romans expanded outward from their ancient homeland near the Tiber. In the space of only a few centuries, they conquered all of Italy, then the lands of the western

Mediterranean, and finally those of the sea's eastern portion. In the process, the balance of power in the known world was completely realigned in Rome's favor. And the city on the Tiber came to control the fates of millions of people who never laid eyes on Rome during their lifetimes.

One important key to this phenomenal success was the efficient and largely productive manner in which Rome expanded its territory and influence. As a rule, after conquering enemies the Romans did not brutalize or destroy them. Instead, they absorbed their opponents one by one, making them part of their growing commonwealth of peoples and states. Often this absorption included treaties that granted former enemies Roman citizenship and legal privileges. In most conquered areas, the Latin language—as well as Roman ideas, laws, and customs—was also introduced, part of an ongoing "Romanization" process.

During the Republic, this process was most methodical, efficient, and successful in Italy itself, the region that came to be seen as the Roman "heartland." Noted scholar Charles Freeman explains:

All [of the conquered peoples] accepted the dominance of Rome and agreed to provide armed support when called upon. Some Latin cities close to Rome lost their independence and were incorporated into the Roman state. . . . The members of these communities became full Roman citizens and could vote in the Roman assemblies. . . . Among the defeated non-Latin communities . . . Rome developed . . . a form of Roman citizenship which involved communities in the obligations of citizenship, notably military service, but without any of the advantages, such as voting. . . . Each of these cities was known as a *municipium*. In the passage of time the citizens of these *municipia* were given full citizenship, the last by the end of the second century B.C. . . . No less crucial were allies. By 250 B.C. Rome had made alliances with over 150 Italian communities who had either been defeated or forced through fear into surrender. Technically the allies maintained full independence, but they had to provide manpower for wars and Rome in effect decided

Etruscan Cultural Influences

Of all the neighboring peoples the early Romans interacted with, none influenced them more than the Etruscans. Rome was sometimes at war with various Etruscan city-states. But when relations between the two peoples were cordial, the Romans borrowed many Etruscan cultural ideas, including artistic styles and skills, architectural concepts (such as the arch, which later became a Roman trademark), and religious, legal, and political concepts. In the late sixth century B.C., for example, Rome began to install stone sewers, a paved forum (main square), and stone temples and other communal buildings, all in imitation of such features in nearby Etruscan cities.

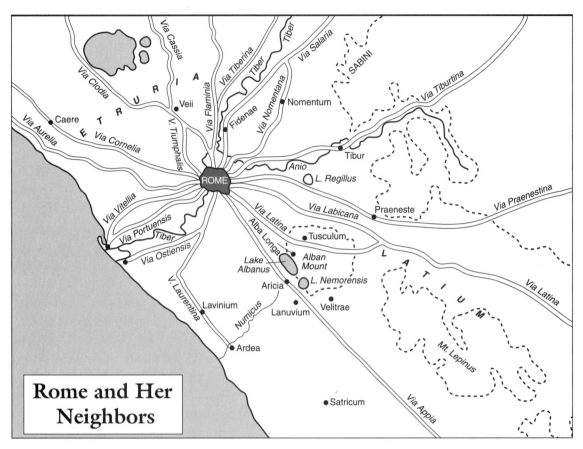

Rome and Her Neighbors

when these wars should take place and how many men were needed.[19]

The Monarchy Overthrown

This mighty process of conquest, alliance, Romanization, and absorption did not get started in earnest until the years immediately following the founding of the Republic. The exact circumstances surrounding this crucial event are unknown. A number of legendary stories were handed down to the later Romans, including one in which the son of the Roman king Tarquin the Proud raped Lucretia, wife of an aristocrat and patriot named Lucius Tarquinius Collatinus; the latter, aided by Lucretia's uncle, Lucius Junius Brutus, then led a coup that ousted the kingship and established the Republic. A number of modern scholars have dismissed these traditions as mere fantasy. However, as T.J. Cornell suggests, this assessment may itself lack foundation. "There is no reason in principle," he writes,

why the tradition should not be a romanticized version of events that really happened. It is arbitrary to

Sextus Tarquinius, son of Rome's king, Tarquin the Proud, rapes Lucretia, daughter of a Roman nobleman, a crime that supposedly set in motion the events of the Monarchy's fall.

dismiss the rape of Lucretia (for instance) as fiction, when we have no way of knowing whether it is fiction or not. The history of many ruling families has been characterized by ruthless brutality and personal tragedy, and . . . the bare catalogue of events within the Tarquin family is, in itself, perfectly credible.[20]

This "bare catalogue of events" began with the tyranny of Tarquin, a man of Etruscan birth who seized the throne after murdering the former king. Tarquin angered the powerful patricians when he arrested several of them on phony charges so that he could grab their wealthy estates

for himself. Collatinus and Brutus were among the Roman notables who came to hate the king. At the same time, Tarquin's equally disreputable son, Sextus, became involved in various intrigues that benefited the ruling family at the expense of the state and citizenry.

Finally, Sextus committed the famous rape that set the revolution in motion. After the crime, Collatinus and Brutus found Lucretia sitting in her room, crying and distressed. She told them about the assault, then added (according to Livy): "My body only has been violated. My heart is innocent, and death will be my witness. Give me your solemn promise that the adulterer shall be punished." The men pledged to seek revenge and then tried to comfort the girl. "They told her she was helpless, and therefore innocent," Livy writes. "It was the mind, they said, that sinned, not the body. Without intention there could never be guilt." Unfortunately, these words did not console Lucretia, who "drew a knife from under her robe, drove it into her heart, and fell forward, dead."[21]

Enraged by Lucretia's mistreatment and death and fed up with the Tarquins' abuses, Brutus, Collatinus, and many other patricians opted to rid the city-state of its corrupt kingship and replace it with a more equitable form of government. This effort seems to have been temporarily hindered by Lars Porsena, king of the Etruscan city of Clusium, northeast of Rome. Around the time the Republic was established, Porsena marched his

Horatius at the Bridge

This is Livy's account (quoted in Livy: The Early History of Rome*) of the Roman hero Horatius's famous defense of the bridge against the invading Etruscans.*

On the approach of the Etruscan army, the Romans abandoned their farmsteads and moved into the city. . . . The most vulnerable point [in the defenses] was the wooden bridge, and the Etruscans would have crossed it and forced an entrance into the city, had it not been for the courage of one man, Horatius Cocles—that great soldier whom the fortune of Rome gave to be her shield on that day of peril. . . . The enemy forces came pouring down the hill, while the Roman troops, throwing away their weapons, were behaving more like undisciplined rabble than a fighting force. Horatius acted promptly. . . . Urging [his comrades] . . . to destroy the bridge by fire or steel or any means they could muster, he offered to hold up the Etruscan advance . . . alone. Proudly he took his stand at the outer edge of the bridge. . . . The advancing enemy paused in sheer astonishment at such reckless courage. . . . With defiance in his eyes Horatius confronted the [enemy], challenging one after the other to single combat. . . . For a while they hung back, each waiting for his neighbor to make the first move until shame . . . drove them to action, and with a fierce cry they hurled their spears at the solitary figure who barred their way. Horatius caught the missiles on his shield and, resolute as ever, straddled the bridge and held his ground. The Etruscans moved forward . . . but their advance was suddenly checked by the crash of the falling bridge. . . . [They] could only stare in bewilderment as Horatius . . . plunged fully armed into the water and swam, through the missiles which fell thick around him, safely to the other side, where his friends were waiting to receive him.

Horatius defends the bridge across the Tiber against the invading Etruscan forces.

army on Rome, intent on sacking it. His invaders encountered a delay at the only bridge then leading across the Tiber, when a Roman patriot named Horatius held them off single-handedly. According to Livy:

> [As] the enemy forces came pouring down the hill . . . Horatius acted promptly. . . . Urging [his comrades] . . . to destroy the bridge by fire or steel or any means they could muster, he offered to hold up the Etruscan advance . . . alone. Proudly he took his stand at the outer edge of the bridge. . . . The advancing enemy paused in sheer astonishment at such reckless courage. . . . With defiance in his eyes Horatius confronted the [enemy], challenging one after the other to single combat.[22]

This story of brave Horatius is one of the quintessential Roman folk stories.

The Major Republican Officials

Despite Horatius's courage, Porsena took the city and made it a base from which to invade other Latin towns lying further south. That prompted these towns to join with the Romans in resisting the Etruscans, who soon met defeat and retreated homeward. The Romans could now concentrate all their energies on setting up their new republican state.

The government of that state retained the old citizen assembly, in which free adult males who owned weapons met to vote on new laws and elect various high magistrates (public officials). These included two consuls serving at the same time; their job was to run the state on a day-to-day basis and to lead the army in wartime. Cicero later described the consuls, the special office of dictator (to be filled in a national emergency), and the important position of praetor, or high judge:

> There shall . . . be two officials with the power that used to belong to the kings. . . . It is "consuls" that they will be habitually called. While on military service they will be invested with supreme authority. There shall be no one above them. Their dominant pre-occupation shall be the welfare of the people. No one [consul] shall occupy the same office twice, except after an interval of ten years duration. . . . When, however, a serious war occurs, or civil strife, a single man shall be invested with the power that normally belongs to the two consuls, if the Senate so decrees. But this dictatorship shall not last longer than six months. . . . The praetor shall be the man who administers justice, and pronounces or guides the verdicts in private lawsuits. It is he who shall be guardian of the civil law. The praetors shall possess equal powers, and there shall be as many of them as the Senate decrees or the assembly ordains.[23]

As for the Senate, its members were mainly patricians and they had the right to keep their positions for life. On paper,

An elderly patron (right front) is aided by his younger client. Clients performed favors for patrons and often accompanied them on public outings.

was a structure composed of powerful *patroni* and their dependent *clientes*. The client was a free man who entrusted himself to the patronage of another and received protection from him in return. The client helped his patron to succeed in public life and furthered his interests by every means in his power, and in return the patron looked after his client's private affairs and gave him financial or legal support. . . . Here was [a] reason why the assembly . . . could never be a truly democratic body. . . . Those assemblymen who lacked wealth were, for the most part, clients of rich men and senators in whose favor . . . they were duty bound to cast their votes in the annual elections to state offices.[24]

this body was still an advisory board to the other leading organs of government (the consuls and assembly). However, in practice, the senators were much more influential. Behind the scenes they often created the political and social agenda enacted by the consuls; also, senators regularly used their wealth and high position to sway members of the assembly to vote in a certain way. They could do this because of a deeply imbedded social system known as patronage. "Roman society," historian Michael Grant explains,

With only occasional exceptions, therefore, the Senate held the overriding political power and authority in the Roman Republic.

A Destiny to Rule

The Republic may not have been a democracy, but it was still a far more progressive and enlightened form of government than most others in the Mediterranean world. Although most Romans had little actual voice in deciding government policy, they benefited immensely by Roman law, which grew increasingly comprehensive and fair over time. The laws protected people of all social classes from the state's abusing their civil rights and reminded them that they were no longer under the arbitrary and corrupt rule of kings. Cicero later summed up the importance of Roman law, saying that it was

> the bond which assures to each of us his honorable life within our commonwealth. It is the foundation of liberty, the fountainhead [main source] of justice. It is what keeps the heart and mind and initiative and feeling of our nation alive. The state without law would be like a body without [a] brain; it could

make no use of its sinews, its blood, or its limbs. The magistrates who administer the law, the judges who act as its spokesmen, [and] all the rest of us who live as its servants, grant it our allegiance as a guarantee of our freedom.[25]

The vast majority of Romans came to feel that this and other benefits of their republican system of government set them apart from other peoples. Roman citizenship was therefore something to be sought after and cherished, and that elicited feelings of pride and patriotism. In fact, many Romans came to believe that the rise of the Republic and the continuing expansion of the territories it controlled were not happy accidents but

Roman troops prepare to lay siege to the citadel of the Etruscan city of Veii in the early fourth century B.C.

preordained events. In this view, the gods were on the Romans' side; as Jupiter stated in Virgil's *Aeneid,* they were a master race whose destiny was to rule the world.

The Conquest of Italy

This rather arrogant attitude grew stronger as, over the course of decades and centuries, Roman armies conquered neighboring peoples and states and steadily increased the extent of Rome's territory and influence. The first major campaign after the formation of the Republic was a victory over the other members of the Latin League, an association of Latin-speaking towns clustered around the plain of Latium. Rome, long an important member of the league, now asserted dominance; and in the years to come, it led the other Latins against their common enemy—the Etruscans. After many years of intermittent fighting, this effort finally prevailed in 396 B.C. as Rome seized the important Etruscan stronghold of Veii. Conquered Etruscan towns retained their local customs and character for a few generations, but over time they were thoroughly absorbed by the ongoing Romanization process.

This cycle of conquest, expansion, and cultural absorption continued in the fourth century B.C. as other Italian towns and peoples were unable to halt the Roman advance. To their credit, the Samnites, who inhabited the valleys of the central and southern Apennines, put up a tremendous fight. At the time that

This modern drawing depicts a Samnite warrior clad in armor. The Romans defeated the Samnites in the third century B.C.

the two peoples came to grips, the lands and population of the Samnites were perhaps twice as big as those of Rome. And like the Romans, the Samnites were aggressive, ambitious, and had strong military traditions.

The first of the three so-called Samnite Wars began in 343 B.C. when the Samnites attacked Capua (in the region of Campania, south of Rome) and ended two years later with the Romans in complete

33

control of northern Campania. In the second war (326–304 B.C.), the Romans suffered a humiliating defeat at the Caudine Forks (near Capua); always resilient, however, they soon bounced back and drove the Samnites out of Campania for good. The Third Samnite War (298–290 B.C.) witnessed a full-scale Roman invasion of the Samnites' mountain heartland. The natives put up a courageous defense but in the end had no choice but surrender.

Roman Conquest of Italy (298–218 B.C.)

0 — 100
Miles

Verona
Mediolanum
Placentia
Mutina
Ariminum
Pisae
Volaterrae · Arretium
Perusia · Ancona
Vetulonia · Volsinii · Firmum
CORSICA · Asculum
Reate
Rome
Ardea · Aesernia · Arpi
Aquinum
Capua · Venusia
SARDINIA
Neapolis · Nola · Tarentum
Metapontum
Thurii
Locri
Rhegium
SICILY

Annexations 241 - 218 B.C.

Roman gains 298 - 263 B.C.

Rome's allies 298 B.C.

Rome's allies 298 - 263 B.C.

Roman and Latin Territory 298 B.C.

Following the defeat of the Samnites, Rome controlled some fifty thousand square miles of territory, probably a hundred times the size of the Roman city-state a mere century before. But Roman expansion did not slow down. During the Samnite conflicts, Roman armies had ventured into the borderlands of the Greek city-states that had grown up across southern Italy in the preceding few centuries. All these city-states controlled valuable farmland and/or ports, and Rome came to view them as tempting targets.

The result was a new stage of Roman expansion that began in 282 B.C. when the Greek city of Thurii asked for Rome to help it repel raids by bands of brigands. The Romans sent ships carrying soldiers. But the neighboring Greek city of Taras (which the Romans called "Tarentum") felt threatened and sank the ships. Rome then sent in its formidable army while the Tarentines called on Pyrrhus, king of the Greek state of Epirus (on the other side of the Adriatic Sea) for help. In 280 B.C. Pyrrhus led a force of more than twenty-two thousand troops against the Romans at Heraclea, near Tarentum. He scored a victory, but it was a costly one. Demonstrating their extraordinary fighting skill and courage, the Romans killed more than a sixth of his army. Pyrrhus fought more bat-

Pyrrhus's Indecisive Campaigns

After defeating the Romans at Heraclea, a colony of Tarentum, in 280 B.C., Pyrrhus marched northward into Latium and got within forty miles of Rome. He realized that to besiege and capture such a large and well-fortified city he would need the aid of many of Rome's local Italian allies, whom the Romans had conquered in the preceding two centuries. When most refused to defect to him, he saw no choice but to head back to southern Italy. Pyrrhus fought the Romans again in 279 B.C. at Ausculum, in southeastern Italy. The tough and stubborn Roman soldiers managed to resist his army for an entire day; but the next day he pushed them back, again with considerable losses to his own forces. This is the moment in which he voiced his now-famous quip that any more victories over Rome would surely be his undoing. Not long afterward, Pyrrhus decided to invade Sicily. It appears that he intended to drive away the Carthaginians who controlled the island; having gained Sicily's resources and manpower, he would then be in a position to fight and defeat both Rome and Carthage. This audacious goal never came to fruition, as Pyrrhus did not fare well during the three years he spent in Sicily. So he returned to Italy in 275 B.C., fought one more indecisive battle against the Romans, and finally sailed for his homeland of Epirus.

tles against the Romans and continued to experience narrow, debilitating wins. Following one of these encounters, he is said to have joked: "One more victory like that over the Romans will destroy us completely!"[26] (Ever since, an excessively costly win has been called a "Pyrrhic victory.")

Finally, Pyrrhus decided to cut his losses and return home. Without his support, none of the Italian Greek cities could hope to stand up to Rome; and within the next few years, all of them acknowledged its dominance in the area.

By 265 B.C. the Romans were the undisputed masters of all Italy south of the Po Valley (the northern region at the foot of the Alps).

The First Punic War

No sooner had Rome gained control of Italy when it began the next stage of its aggressive expansion, one that would put it in a dominant position over the seaways and coasts of the western Mediterranean sphere. The main target was the empire of Carthage, centered in what is now Tunisia, in North Africa. Before leaving Italy for

Epirus, Pyrrhus had said: "My friends, what a wrestling ground we are leaving behind us for the Romans and Carthaginians."[27] This turned out to be a truly prophetic remark. Rome now embarked on the three Punic Wars, the largest, bloodiest conflicts fought anywhere in the world up to that time. (The term "Punic" comes from the Latin name for Phoenician; the Phoenicians, a maritime people from the eastern Mediterranean, were the original founders of Carthage.)

The First Punic War began in 264 B.C. when Carthage occupied Messina, on the northeastern tip of the island of Sicily, only a few miles from the southern Italian shore. The Romans quickly declared war. But they knew they had a problem,

namely, that the Carthaginians had a powerful navy, while Rome had virtually no war fleets. Incredibly, the Romans constructed a fleet of 120 warships in only a few months, then boldly challenged the Carthaginians.

In the ensuing battles, the Romans won several victories, which surprised observers around the Mediterranean world even more than Rome's feat of building the ships. Part of the credit for the Roman success goes to a secret weapon they employed. Called the *corvus*, meaning "raven," it was a wooden gangway that stood upright on the deck until it crashed down onto the deck of an enemy ship and held it fast, allowing Roman soldiers to board and fight hand-to-hand. This de-

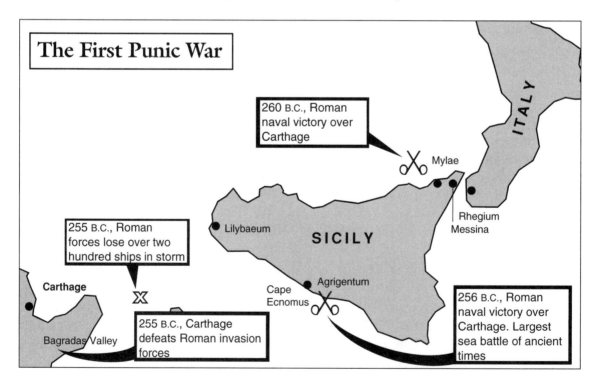

The First Punic War

260 B.C., Roman naval victory over Carthage — Mylae

255 B.C., Roman forces lose over two hundred ships in storm

256 B.C., Roman naval victory over Carthage. Largest sea battle of ancient times

255 B.C., Carthage defeats Roman invasion forces

Carthage
Bagradas Valley
Lilybaeum
SICILY
Cape Ecnomus
Agrigentum
Rhegium
Messina
ITALY

An Extraordinary Spirit and Audacity

From 264 to 241, Rome and Carthage grappled in the most devastating war fought anywhere in the world up to that time. Rome won this so-called First Punic War in large degree because it took the bold step of creating its very first fleet of warships, a feat accomplished in only sixty days. This was a classic demonstration of the Romans' renowned practicality, resourcefulness, and determination. According to the second-century B.C. Greek historian Polybius (in his Histories*), it was*

because they saw that the war was dragging on that they first applied themselves to building ships—[120 warships in all]. They faced great difficulties because their shipwrights were completely inexperienced in the building of [warships]. . . . Yet it is this fact which illustrates better than any other the extraordinary spirit and audacity of the Romans' decision. It was not a question of having adequate resources for the enterprise, for they had in fact none whatsoever, nor had they ever given a thought to the sea before this. But once they had conceived the idea, they embarked on it so boldly, that without waiting to gain any experience in naval warfare they immediately engaged the Carthaginians, who had for generations enjoyed an unchallenged supremacy at sea.

The Romans constructed warships like these in large numbers at the start of their first war with Carthage.

vice, along with sheer daring and tenacity, gave the Romans victories in the huge sea battles of Mylae (260 B.C.) and Cape Ecnomus (256 B.C.).

Next the Romans landed an army in North Africa in an attempt to capture Carthage. This force met defeat, however, after which several violent storms sank hundreds of Roman warships. Upward of 200,000 Roman soldiers and sailors died, the worse naval losses of one nation in a single war in history. To the foreign observers still watching with interest, Rome appeared to be on the brink of total ruin. Yet as they had in the past and would again in the future, the Romans showed their amazing stubbornness, courage, and resilience. They pooled all their remaining resources, built still another fleet, and hammered the enemy into submission in 241 B.C. The humiliated Carthaginians sued for peace, and Rome gained control over the large islands of Sicily and Sardinia.

Rome's Darkest Hour

The Second Punic War was even larger and more devastating than the first. It began in 218 B.C., soon after the Carthaginian leader Hannibal attacked Saguntum, a Roman ally on Spain's eastern coast. Hannibal, who turned out to be one of the greatest military generals in history, surprised the Romans by crossing his army over the Alps and entering northern Italy. In the months that followed, he won stunning victories at the Trebia River and Lake Trasimene and threatened the Roman heartland.

Hannibal's greatest victory of all came in 216 B.C. at Cannae, in southeastern Italy, where the Romans suffered their worst single battlefield loss ever. Hannibal lured two consuls and their huge army into a trap and slaughtered more than fifty thousand of them, with losses of only about eight thousand in his own ranks. It was truly Rome's darkest

Hannibal's Campaign Against Rome (218–216 B.C.)

218 B.C., Battle of Trebia

217 B.C., Battle of Lake Trasimene

216 B.C., Battle of Cannae

Po

Ticinus River

Trebia

CORSICA

Rome

Capua

SARDINIA

TYRRHENIAN SEA

ADRIATIC SEA

Carthage

SICILY

hour. Livy described the mood in Rome on hearing news of the disaster:

Never, without an enemy actually within the gates, had there been such terror and confusion in the city. . . . Two consular armies annihilated . . . Rome left without a force in the field . . . nearly the whole of Italy overrun. No other nation in the world could have suffered so tremendous a series of disasters and not been overwhelmed. It was unparalleled in history.[28]

Yet Rome was not overwhelmed. Once more the Romans turned what seemed like certain defeat into decisive victory. Hannibal failed to follow up his win at Cannae by marching on Rome and soon found it impossible to persuade Rome's Italian allies to defect to him. In 202 B.C. the Romans carried the war to Africa, forcing Hannibal to leave Italy. That same year, on the plain of Zama, not far from Carthage, the Roman general Publius Cornelius Scipio (later called Africanus) delivered Hannibal his first and only defeat. Once more humiliated, the Carthaginians were forced to cede Spain and most of their other territories to Rome.

"Our Sea"

During the years the Romans and Carthaginians battled for supremacy in the western Mediterranean, most of the Greek kingdoms and city-states in the sea's western sphere watched and waited. But apparently few of the Greeks grasped the danger that Rome's faraway victories posed to them. An exception was the orator Agelaus of Aetolia (a federation of Greek cities), who warned in 213 B.C.:

Let me impress on you how important it is . . . that we should consult one another and remain on our guard,

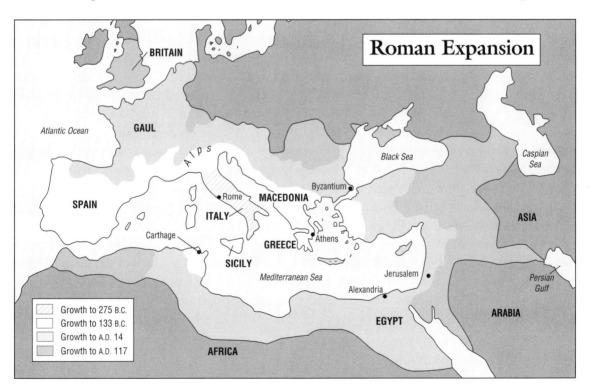

Roman Expansion

Growth to 275 B.C.
Growth to 133 B.C.
Growth to A.D. 14
Growth to A.D. 117

in view of the huge armies which have been mobilized, and vast scale of the war [the Second Punic War] which is now being waged in the west. For it must already be obvious to all those who pay even the slightest attention to affairs of state that whether the Carthaginians defeat the Romans or the Romans the Carthaginians, the victors will by no means be satisfied with the sovereignty of Italy and Sicily, but will come here [to Greece], and will advance both their forces and their ambitions beyond the bounds of justice.[29]

Only a year after the close of the Second Punic War (201 B.C.), Agelaus's dire prediction came true with a vengeance. During that huge conflict, Philip V, king of the Greek kingdom of Macedonia, had made an alliance with Carthage. No doubt he, like so many others, had expected Hannibal to win, a grave miscalculation. In 200 B.C. the Romans unleashed their retribution on Philip by launching the Second Macedonian War. (The First Macedonian War was Rome's designation for the help Philip had given Hannibal.) In 197 B.C., at Cynoscephalae ("Dog's Heads"), in central Greece, Philip went down to defeat, losing 8,000 dead and 5,000 captured, while the Romans lost only 700 men. In this single stroke, the Roman army had shown its superiority to the finest military machine Greece had to offer.

Indeed, the results of the battles and wars that followed between the Romans and Greeks were little different than that of Cynoscephalae. In 189 B.C. the Romans crushed Antiochus III, ruler of the Greek Seleucid kingdom (encompassing much of what are now Iraq and Turkey). Then came the Third Macedonian War (171–168 B.C.). The Romans easily defeated Philip's son, Perseus, and a few years later liquidated the Macedonian kingdom and made it a Roman province.

Finally, in 146 B.C. Greece's Achaean League (an alliance of cities in southern Greece) staged a courageous but ultimately futile resistance against the encroaching Romans. To teach the losers, as well as any would-be rebels, a lesson, Rome razed the once-great city of Corinth to the ground. That same year an army commanded by the Roman general Scipio Aemilianus wiped Carthage from the map in a similar manner. The Roman Republic's great war machine and long orgy of expansion now came to a temporary rest. The wide Mediterranean had become a Roman lake, which many Romans now came to call *mare nostrum,* "our sea." No one then living could have foreseen that only a century later, the mighty Republic, whose armies had conquered much of the known world, would be in its death throes.

Fall of the Republic and Rise of the Empire

That the Roman Republic was a strong and effective political entity is proven by its longevity and many political, social, and military successes. However, Rome's republican government had some serious structural weaknesses that became increasingly obvious and ominous as the Roman commonwealth grew larger and more complex. First, the very task of governing became more and more difficult. Rome's political institutions and customs and most of its laws had been initially designed to govern a single city-state inhabited by one people. On the scale of an empire encompassing many diverse peoples, the system did not work nearly as well.

Another weakness of the system was military in nature. Rome certainly had the benefit of large, well-disciplined armies and highly skilled generals. However, the republican state had a long-standing policy of failing to reward its troops with pensions and land upon their retirement. Filling this vacuum, so to speak, a number of leading generals began using their considerable wealth and influence to supply their soldiers with such benefits. Not surprisingly, trouble began to brew when these soldiers started feeling more loyal to their generals than to the government.

According to the second-century A.D. Greek historian Appian, the troops often "felt they were not so much serving in the army as lending assistance from personal goodwill and by their own choice . . .

[to leaders who needed them] to attain their private ends."[30] In a passage from his monumental *Roman Revolution*, the late historian Ronald Syme added:

> The soldiers, now recruited from the poorest classes in Italy, were ceasing to feel allegiance to the state; military service was for livelihood . . . not a natural and normal part of a citizen's duty. The necessities of a world empire and the ambition of generals led to the creation of extraordinary commands [armies following their generals] in the provinces. The general had to be a politician, for his legionaries were a host of clients, looking to their leader for spoils in war and estates in Italy when their campaigns were over. . . . Such were the resources which ambition required to win power in Rome and direct the policy of the imperial Republic.[31]

In trying to "direct the policy" of the government, this new breed of ambitious generals inevitably ended up amassing great political power and challenging the government's authority. The first of these military leaders to create his own personal army was Gaius Marius; born in 157 B.C., he became a national hero by defeating a force of Germanic invaders and served as consul seven times. In time he carried on a policy of arranging for his retired veterans to receive generous land allotments in northern Africa, southern Gaul, Sicily, and Greece. Later many of

A drawing of a statue of Gaius Marius, a military hero who served as consul seven times.

these men helped him in his political struggles, sometimes committing violent acts against his enemies.

Taking their cue from Marius, in the years that followed, other generals raised personal armies and manipulated the state, among them Cornelius Sulla, Gnaeus

Pompey, Julius Caesar, and Mark Antony. These and other ambitious individuals squared off in a series of enormously destructive civil wars that eventually caused the collapse of the Republic and its ideals of representative government.

In the Republic's place rose a more autocratic form of government—the Roman Empire. It was largely the creation of Octavian, Julius Caesar's adopted son. Renamed Augustus, "the revered one," he became its first and greatest emperor (though he never actually used this title)

and set many precedents for the new Roman age that he initiated.

Marius Versus Sulla

The first civil discord in the series of events leading to the downfall of the Republic and rise of the Empire involved Marius and Sulla. The two had once been military associates; but later, in the political arena, they became opponents. Marius, who had been born a commoner and risen through the ranks, had acquired the support of everyday Romans,

Sulla, the first Roman general to march his army on Rome, fights his way through the city's streets. He was victorious and declared himself dictator.

Sulla's Lists of the Condemned

In this excerpt from his Life of Sulla *(in* Fall of the Roman Republic*), Plutarch describes Sulla's brutal political purges.*

The city was filled with murder and there was no counting the executions or setting a limit to them. Many people were killed because of purely personal ill feeling; they had no connection with Sulla in any way, but Sulla, in order to gratify members of his own party, permitted them to be done away with. . . . Without consulting any magistrate, Sulla published a list of eighty men to be condemned. Public opinion was horrified, but, after a single day's interval, he published another list containing 220 more names, and the next day a third list with the same number of names on it. And in a public speech . . . he said that he was publishing the names of all those whom he happened to remember: those who escaped his memory for the moment would have their names put up later. He also condemned anyone who sheltered or attempted to save a person whose name was on the lists. Death was the penalty for such acts of humanity, and there were no exceptions in the cases of brothers, sons, or parents.

who respected him as a self-made man and looked on him as their champion. In contrast, Sulla was a patrician and backed the interests of Rome's aristocratic and wealthy factions.

In 88 B.C. Sulla rose to the office of consul, and the Senate appointed him to take an army to Asia Minor, where hostile forces had invaded a Roman province. However, the leaders of the popular party, who dominated the people's assembly, did not want an aristocrat to get this prestigious assignment. They preferred that Marius go to Asia Minor. As the mood in the capital turned ugly, Sulla decided to act in his and his party's interests. He marched his troops into Rome, the first time a consul had ever used force to gain mastery of the city. When he was satisfied that his supporters were firmly in control, he led his troops off toward Asia Minor.

Once Sulla had departed, the popular party struck back. Fighting between the opposing factions broke out in the streets, and eventually Marius joined the fray at the head of his own troops. Many aristocrats were killed. Soon afterward Marius, who was by now in his seventies, died suddenly, but his supporters carried on the fight when Sulla returned from the East in 83 B.C. Sulla marched on Rome a second time and defeated his opponents at the city gates.

Sulla now took another unprecedented action. He made himself dictator, usurping a right that had long rested with the Senate alone. He also initiated a series of bloody purges of Marius's supporters and their families. "Sulla now devoted himself entirely to the work of butchery," Plutarch later wrote. "The city was filled with murder and there was no counting the executions or setting a limit to them." In addition to members of the popular party, the dictator's victims included several well-to-do people, including aristocrats, which surprised and worried many in Sulla's own party. His motivation for this outrage was the acquisition of money and property to give his troops and thereby keep their loyalty. According to Plutarch: "It became a regular thing to say among the executioners that 'So-and-so was killed by his big mansion, so-and-so by his gardens, [and] so-and-so by his hot-water installation [private baths].'"[32]

The Rivalry of Pompey and Crassus

Fortunately for Rome, Sulla's abuse of state power was short-lived. In 78 B.C. he died, and the government and capital city soon returned to normal, at least on the surface. Beneath that calm surface, however, the process of decay was already at work. Marius, Sulla, and their round of

civil strife had set a dangerous precedent and shown how ambitious men could use wealth, military power, and political influence to manipulate and even subvert the government.

This ominous lesson was not lost on a new group of military strongmen who achieved notoriety and power in the decades following Sulla's death. Pompey was the first of these men to gain prominence. Originally one of Sulla's inner circle, he earned a reputation as a daring and able soldier and became popular with many senators and other aristocrats. The Senate liked Pompey so much that in 77 B.C. it

A bust of Pompey, who began to gain prominence after the death of Sulla.

sent him to Spain to put down a revolt led by one of Marius's former supporters. In the four years that followed, Pompey was quite successful and his name became a household word back in Rome.

Meanwhile, another influential Roman, the wealthy financier Marcus Crassus, felt himself overshadowed by Pompey's growing reputation. About the jealousy Crassus felt toward Pompey, Plutarch wrote:

> He was much annoyed by Pompey's successes as a commander, by the triumph [victory parade] which he held before becoming a senator, and by the

Marcus Crassus, the wealthy Roman who defeated the slave army commanded by Spartacus.

title of "Magnus," or "The Great," which he received from his fellow citizens. On one occasion when someone said: "Pompey the Great is coming," Crassus merely laughed and asked, "As great as what?" Giving up, therefore, all attempts to equal Pompey in military matters, Crassus devoted himself to politics.[33]

Fortune soon smiled on Crassus, however. While Pompey was still away in Spain, a crisis arose that allowed Crassus to fulfill his greatest desire—to take command of an army. In 73 B.C. a group of gladiators at a training school in Capua (about a hundred miles south of Rome) escaped and began terrorizing the surrounding countryside. Led by a gladiator named Spartacus, the escapees trained a number of runaway slaves to fight and defeated several small Roman armies sent against them. Deeply worried, the Senate agreed to entrust Crassus with the task of putting down the rebellion.

At first, Crassus's campaign achieved little success. So the Senate recalled his rival, Pompey, from Spain to help, which obviously greatly annoyed and worried Crassus. According to Plutarch, Crassus knew "that the credit for the success would be likely to go not to himself but to the commander who appeared on the scene with reinforcements"; so "he made all haste he could to finish the war"[34] before Pompey arrived.

Crassus did manage to attack and defeat Spartacus in 71 B.C. However, just

Crassus Defeats Spartacus

The final battle in Crassus's campaign against the rebels led by Spartacus took place late in 71 B.C. near the Silarus River, in southern Italy. In this tract from his Life of Crassus *(in* Fall of the Roman Republic*), Plutarch claims that Spartacus personally tried to kill Crassus.*

When [Spartacus's] horse was brought to him, he drew his sword and killed it, saying that the enemy had plenty of good horses which would be his if he won, and, if he lost, he would not need a horse at all. Then he made straight for Crassus himself, charging forward through the press of weapons and wounded men, and, though he did not reach Crassus, he cut down two centurions [unit leaders] who fell on [attacked] him together. Finally, when his own men had taken to flight, he himself, surrounded by enemies, still stood his ground and died fighting to the last.

as he had feared, Pompey showed up just in time to take most of the credit for the victory.

Cicero, Caesar, and the First Triumvirate

Because of their success in putting down the slave uprising, for a short while Crassus and Pompey were the most famous men in Rome. Pompey received even more adulation when, in 67 B.C., he rid the entire Mediterranean Sea of pirates in only forty days. Two other prominent men soon emerged to challenge Crassus and Pompey, however. One of them, Caesar, was an ambitious, power-hungry person like themselves; the other, the orator, lawyer, and statesman Cicero, was an ardent champion of republican gov-

ernment and the rule of law. If Pompey, Crassus, and Caesar were to have any chance of dominating the state, sooner or later they would have to confront and deal with Cicero.

Cicero was already widely popular and respected in Rome when he won the consular election of 63 B.C., in which he courageously opposed the candidates supported by Crassus. No sooner had Cicero assumed his office, when he exposed and foiled a military plot to murder the consuls and overthrow the government. This made him a heroic figure in the eyes of most Romans. On his way home from the Senate, Plutarch wrote:

People shouted aloud and clapped their hands, calling him the savior . . .

Julius Caesar (left), who organized the First Triumvirate, and Cicero, who served as consul and senator and was later hailed as Rome's greatest orator.

of his country. . . . The Roman people owed thanks to many commanders and generals of the time for riches and spoils and power, but for the safety and security of the whole, their thanks were due to Cicero and Cicero alone, who had delivered them from this great and terrible danger.[35]

Cicero's moment of power and influence was fleeting, however. In the same year that he won the consulship, Caesar was elected praetor, or high judge. In his own recent climb up the traditional ladder of government offices, Caesar had already begun to show considerable political skills. Sometimes, he realized, it was necessary to make deals with one's opponents in order to further one's immediate aims; so it made sense to work

with Pompey and Crassus against Cicero and the Senate. Accordingly, in the summer of 60 B.C., Caesar formed a secret pact with Pompey and Crassus, a powerful partnership that later came to be called the First Triumvirate ("rule of three"). The triumvirs knew that each, by himself, lacked the resources to challenge the Senate. But by combining their wealth and influence, they had an even chance of manipulating the government to serve their own needs and ambitions.

The triumvirs wasted no time in implementing their scheme. Backed by Pompey, Crassus, and their many supporters, Caesar easily won the next consular election. Serving as consul in 59 B.C., he regularly intimidated his political opponents, brokered shady deals, ignored or broke various laws, and used the threat of force to silence dissent. Meanwhile, said Plutarch, Pompey

filled the Forum with armed men and helped the people to pass Caesar's laws. . . . Out of the whole number of senators, only a very few used to attend the meetings presided over by Caesar; the rest showed their hatred of his proceedings by staying away.[36]

Cicero had long worried that the rise of powerful, ruthless individuals might threaten or even destroy the state. Now, the dangerous actions of the triumvirs proved that his fears had not been misplaced.

Caesar's Civil War and Dictatorship

Indeed, Caesar's attainment of the office of consul marked only the beginning of

Pompey Rids the Sea of Pirates

Pompey became a national hero by eliminating the pirates who had come to menace Mediterranean shipping. As Plutarch tells it in his Life of Pompey (in Fall of the Roman Republic), *the extraordinary operation destroyed some thirteen hundred pirate vessels and captured four hundred more, all without the loss of a single Roman ship.*

The power of the pirates extended over the whole area of our Mediterranean sea. The result was that all navigation and all commerce were at a standstill; and it was this aspect of the situation which caused the Romans . . . to send out Pompey with a commission to drive the pirates off the seas. . . . Pompey was to be given not only the supreme naval command but what amounted in fact to an absolute authority and uncontrolled power over everyone. The law provided that his command should extend over the sea as far as the pillars of Hercules [Strait of Gibraltar] and over all the mainland to the distance of fifty miles from the sea. . . . Then he was . . . given power to . . . take from the treasury and from the taxation officials as much money as he wanted, to raise a fleet of 200 ships, and to arrange personally for the levying of troops and sailors in whatever numbers he thought fit. . . . He divided the Mediterranean and the adjacent coasts into thirteen separate areas, each of which he entrusted to a commander with a fixed number of ships. This disposal of his forces throughout the sea enabled him to surround entire fleets of pirate ships, which he hunted down and brought into harbor. . . . All this was done in the space of forty days.

his ambitions. Following his consulship, he became governor of the province of Transalpine Gaul (now southern France). This was an important and well-calculated move because a governor had instant access to an army to guard his province, and Caesar fully realized he needed military experience and the allegiance of troops to increase his clout in the ongoing power struggle. With this in mind, between 58 and 51 B.C., he conquered the still-wild lands of central and northern Gaul. Besides gaining the loyalty of tens of thousands of battle-hardened troops, Plutarch stated,

> he took by storm more than 800 cities [actually villages], subdued 300 nations [tribes and other local groups], and fought pitched battles at various times with three million men, of whom he destroyed one million in actual fighting and took another million prisoners.[37]

These figures are almost certainly exaggerations. But there is no doubt that Caesar accomplished the personal goals he had set and made himself the strongest and most feared leader in the Roman realm.

Indeed, by 50 B.C. Crassus was dead (having been killed in a military campaign in the East) and Pompey had become the tool of senators who had turned him against Caesar in an effort to shatter the rest of the Triumvirate. In another move designed to weaken Caesar, in January 49 B.C. the Senate ordered him to disband his army at once. As might

be expected, Caesar refused. He knew that the consequence of his refusal might be civil war, but he welcomed it as his biggest challenge yet. On January 7, in open defiance of the government, he led his troops to the Rubicon River, the formal boundary between the Gallic provinces and Italy proper, and told his men: "We may still draw back, but, once across that little bridge, we shall have to fight it out. . . . Let us accept [the signs] from the gods, and follow where they beckon, in vengeance on our double-dealing enemies. The die is cast."[38]

The war that ensued was destined to catapult Caesar to the pinnacle of power in Rome. As he marched on the capital, Pompey, along with many senators, fled to Greece and swiftly raised an army. Caesar and Pompey clashed the following year on the plain of Pharsalus (in east-central Greece), and for the first time in his long career, Pompey tasted defeat. Fleeing again, this time to Egypt, Pompey attempted to take refuge with the young king of that country, Ptolemy XIII. Unfortunately for him, Ptolemy and his advisers feared Caesar, and hoping to gain his favor, they murdered Pompey. To their surprise, however, when Caesar arrived in Egypt, he was horrified and angry that his old colleague had been treated so brutally. He sided with Ptolemy's sister, Cleopatra VII, in an ongoing power struggle for the Egyptian throne; soon, thanks to Caesar, Ptolemy was dead and Cleopatra was queen and firmly in control of the country.

Slaves carry Caesar's mutilated corpse from the Senate House. The dictator's death left a power vacuum that other ambitious men were quick to fill.

Caesar eventually returned to Rome. There he made the mistake of declaring himself dictator for life and accepting religious dedications that referred to him as a god. At this point, the Republic was all but dead; however, a group of senators led by Gaius Cassius and Marcus Brutus believed that they could restore its power and prestige by getting rid of Caesar. They stabbed him to death in the Senate on March 15, 44 B.C., then ran into the streets proclaiming liberty.

Enter Antony and Octavian

But Caesar's grisly murder did not restore the conspirators' beloved Republic. A new generation of ambitious men, including Caesar's hard-drinking lieutenant, Antony, and adopted son, Octavian, quickly moved to fill the vacuum

Antony (top center) reveals Caesar's dead body to a Roman crowd. Shortly afterward, the angry mob went after the assassins.

customary eulogy over it in the Forum. When he saw that his oratory had cast a spell over the people and that they were deeply stirred by his words, he began to introduce into his praises a note of pity and of indignation at Caesar's fate. Finally, at the close of his speech, he snatched up the dead man's robe and brandished it aloft, all blood-stained as it was and stabbed through in many places, and called those who had done the deed murderers and villains. This appeal had such an effect on the people that they piled up benches and tables and burned Caesar's body in the Forum, and then, snatching up firebrands from the pyre, they ran to the houses of his assassins and attacked them.[39]

created by the dictator's demise. In fact, the conspirators immediately found themselves in deep trouble, partly because they had failed to anticipate Antony's ability to sway the Roman mob against them. At first, he pretended to support them so as to put them off their guard. Then he struck his first blow. "It so happened," Plutarch wrote in his biography of Antony,

> that when Caesar's body was carried out for burial, Antony delivered the

Fearing for their lives, the conspirators fled Rome and most of them ended up in Greece, where they began raising troops to fight Antony.

Antony was now the most powerful figure in Rome. Cicero was still around. But he knew that Antony hated him and also distrusted the Senate. Rather than risk provoking Antony into assassinating the remaining republican leadership, Cicero and his colleagues decided to lay low for the time being. They watched with interest when, about two months after Caesar's death, the nineteen-year-old Octavian showed up in the capital to claim Caesar's inheritance. Antony made the mistake of dismissing the youth as too weak and inexperienced to cause him any trouble. But Octavian was shrewd and calculating far beyond his years. He proceeded to hire some three thousand of Caesar's veteran soldiers and to promise Cicero that he would use these troops to defend the Senate against Antony. Realizing that he had been outmaneuvered, Antony retired to northern Italy.

Octavian now also outmaneuvered Cicero and the Senate, who had underestimated him as much as Antony had. The young man demanded that the senators make him consul and marched his small army into Rome to make it clear that he meant business. Seeing that they really had no other choice, the senators complied.

The Second Triumvirate

Octavian now found himself at a fateful juncture. He was not foolish enough to think that he could maintain his dominance

The three members of the Second Triumvirate—Octavian, Antony, and Lepidus—meet in 43 B.C. One of their first acts was to make a hit list of their enemies.

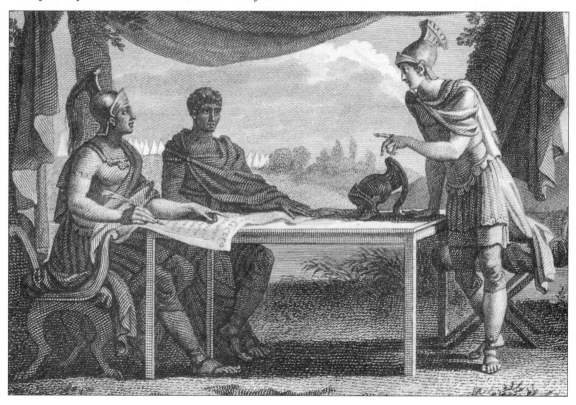

in Rome indefinitely with a small force of soldiers. Antony was presently raising troops of his own in the north; other military factions, the strongest led by a general named Marcus Lepidus, were poised to enter the power struggle; and Brutus's and Cassius's republican forces were steadily gaining strength in Greece.

Facing the suicidal prospect of fighting so many strong and diverse factions, Octavian followed Caesar's example and made a deal with his main opponents. In the winter of 43 B.C., Octavian formed a new triumvirate with Antony and Lepidus, and the three arrogantly divided up the Roman realm among themselves. According to Appian:

> The three sat together in council, Octavian in the center because he was consul. They were in conference from morning till night for two days, and came to [the decision] . . . that a distribution of the [Roman] provinces should be made, giving Antony the whole of Gaul. . . . Spain was assigned to Lepidus, while Octavian was to have Africa, Sardinia, and Sicily. . . . Only the assignment of the parts beyond the Adriatic [i.e., in the East] was postponed, since these were still under the control of Brutus and Cassius, against whom Antony and Octavian were to wage war.[40]

The new triumvirs also agreed to exterminate their main political rivals and enemies. As Sulla had done two generations before, they composed a list of "enemies of the state" and instituted a bloody purge that eliminated many Romans still loyal to the Republic. Cicero's name appeared first on Antony's list. Learning of the danger, the aging senator fled to the seacoast south of Rome in hopes of boarding a ship bound for Greece. But before he could escape, Antony's henchmen caught up with him. In a display of unnecessary barbarity, they severed his head, which Antony ordered nailed to a platform in Rome's Forum.

The next order of business for the triumvirs was to deal with Brutus and Cassius, who had managed to raise more than eighty thousand troops still loyal to the Republic. The opposing forces met in October 42 B.C. on the plain of Philippi, in northern Greece. Antony and Octavian were victorious; and rather than surrender, the humiliated former conspirators committed suicide, taking with them the last realistic chance of restoring the Republic.

Octavian Versus Antony and Cleopatra

As had been the case with so many other powerful factions vying for ultimate power in Rome, the triumph of the Second Triumvirate was short-lived. Like the first such alliance of ambitious men, this one now quickly fell apart.

First Octavian and Antony pushed the weaker Lepidus aside, placing him under permanent house arrest. Then the remaining two triumvirs came to death grips in still another civil war. Antony formed a power base in the eastern Mediterranean and became both ally and lover of Egypt's Queen Cleopatra, who supplied vast resources of money and grain for the war effort. Meanwhile, Octavian, defending Italy and the western provinces, launched a clever and effective propaganda campaign. He portrayed Cleopatra as a disreputable, sneaky character whose goal was to rule over Rome. Antony was painted as a weak-willed, naïve person who had allowed the nefarious queen to trick him into betraying his country.

In September, 31 B.C., Octavian followed up this verbal attack with armed action. His friend Marcus Agrippa, a talented military commander, engineered the defeat of Antony and Cleopatra in a large naval encounter at Actium, in western Greece. At the height of the fighting, the lovers fled and made their way back to Egypt's capital, Alexandria. There, the following year, as Octavian closed in on them, they took their own lives, leaving him, at the age of thirty-two, the most powerful figure in the Mediterranean world.

Dying from a self-inflicted wound, Antony is raised to Cleopatra, who has shut herself in her own tomb. Soon, she also committed suicide.

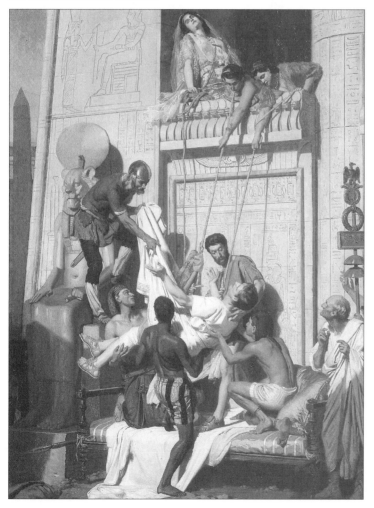

Birth of the Principate

Like Caesar, Octavian wanted to replace the Republic with one-man rule, essentially a benign dictatorship. But the younger man was wise enough not to repeat his father's principal mistake. Caesar had simply declared himself absolute dictator in open contempt of the old republican ideals and institutions. Octavian realized that his best course was

Augustus Saluted as Father of His Country

Here, from his Lives of the Twelve Caesars, *Suetonius tells how the Romans, grateful to Augustus (formerly Octavian) for bringing them peace, honored him with the title of* pater patriae.

In a universal movement to confer on Augustus the title "Father of His Country," the first approach was made by the commons [members of the people's assembly]. . . . When he declined this honor a huge crowd met him outside the Theater with laurel wreaths, and repeated the request. Finally, the Senate followed suit . . . [and] chose Valerius Messala to speak for them all. . . . Messala's words were: "Caesar Augustus, I am instructed to wish you and your family good fortune and divine blessings; which amounts to wishing that our entire State will be fortunate and our country prosperous. The Senate agrees with the people of Rome in saluting you as Father of Your Country." With tears in his eyes, Augustus answered . . . "Fathers of the Senate, I have at last achieved my highest ambition. What more can I ask of the immortal gods than that they may permit me to enjoy your approval until my dying day?"

instead to utilize those old traditions, to manipulate them to his own advantage and thereby gain the backing of all factions.

Working in Octavian's favor was the fact that the Roman people were tired of the suffering, destruction, and uncertainty of decades of civil wars. And they longed for the return of more peaceful times. To gain that tranquillity, he reasoned, they would probably agree to the rule of a single powerful individual, as long as he was fair, law-abiding, and loyal to Roman ideals and customs.

Octavian's challenge, therefore, was to retain the great power he had recently ac-quired without doing away with the offices and symbols of the old republican system. He kept the Senate and consuls, for example, though they now held little actual power and largely answered to him. As the second-century Roman historian Dio Cassius put it, on paper the Republic still existed, while in reality "the power both of the people and of the Senate was wholly transferred into [Octavian's] hands."[41]

Moreover, the old system had venerated the image of ordinary Romans showing their patriotism by serving the state, and through it the Roman people, in various public offices. So Octavian now began reshaping his own image as that of a simple man of the people, a fair leader who respected the law, tradition, and religion, and cared about the well-being of the people. A close friend, the wealthy literary patron Gaius Maecenas, is reported to have told him:

> How can men fail to regard you with affection as their father and their savior, when they see that you are both disciplined and principled in your life, formidable in war and yet disposed to peace, that you show no arrogance and take no advantage . . . [and] do not live in luxury while imposing hardships on others?[42]

Thus, in the months and years that followed, Octavian slowly consolidated a wide array of powers, always in a manner that did not appear to violate established Roman law and tradition. He did not confer any lofty titles on himself. In fact, there was no need to do so, since the senators did it for him; on January 16, 27 B.C., they thanked him for "saving the country" and declared that hereafter he would bear the majestic title of Augustus, meaning "the revered one." He insisted that he was only the Princeps, or "First Citizen." But this was clearly a combination of political spin and false modesty. Despite the republican trappings with which he surrounded himself, Augustus was nothing less an emperor; and the new political entity over which he presided—the Principate (meaning "rule of the First Citizen")—was nothing less than an empire.

Chapter
4

The Pax Romana: Rome at Its Zenith

Like Sulla, Caesar, and other Roman strongmen before him, Octavian had risen to ultimate power through lawlessness, violence, and other ruthless means. One might have expected that now, as Augustus, with all of the government institutions within his grasp, he would become a cruel despot and rule with an iron fist. However, essentially the opposite happened. In his forty-four-year reign, which came to be called the Augustan Age in his honor, Augustus used his great powers almost exclusively in constructive, beneficial ways. He created a police force and fire brigade for the capital city; reformed both the administration of the provinces and the tax system; built dozens of temples, theaters,

and other public buildings; and was so vigorous in his support of the arts and literature that his reign came to encompass Rome's greatest artistic and literary golden age.

Moreover, Augustus's reign provided the foundation of one of history's most remarkable ages. A majority of his immediate successors were thoughtful, effective rulers who brought peace and economic stability to the Roman world. During the Empire's first two centuries, therefore, the Mediterranean sphere experienced an extraordinary degree of peace and prosperity, so much so that it later became known as the Pax Romana, or "Roman Peace." The period also witnessed Roman civilization reach its zenith

Rome's Campus Martius sector as it looked in the second century A.D. *During the Augustan Age, Rome was transformed from a dirty and chaotic city into a clean and orderly capital.*

in size, political influence, and cultural productivity.

Revitalizing the Capital

One of the first and most important of the Pax Romana's productive and constructive aspects was the transformation of the imperial capital itself. Before the Augustan Age, Rome was a largely dirty, chaotic, and unattractive city that regularly experienced floods, fires, building collapses, and other disasters. Livy, a contemporary of Augustus, remarked:

Nobody bothered to see that the streets were straight . . . [and] buildings went up wherever there was room for them. This explains why the ancient sewers, which originally followed the line of the streets, now run in many places under private houses, and why the general layout of Rome is more like a squatters' settlement than a properly planned city.[43]

Augustus must have felt that his new imperial order needed a more presentable capital, one that would become a suitable centerpiece for Rome's "superior" civilization. So the Princeps instigated a large-scale program of rebuilding and revitalization, as well as new construction. The first-century A.D. Roman historian Suetonius later wrote:

Aware that the city was architecturally unworthy of her position as capital of

Overhauling the Capital's Water System

Augustus assigned the major task of aqueduct construction to his trusted friend Marcus Agrippa, who became in effect Rome's first permanent water commissioner. In prior years, four aqueducts had flowed into the city. Now that Rome's population was approaching a million, their combined output was not enough to supply all the water needed for drinking, cooking, washing, and flushing refuse through the sewers. So Agrippa erected two new ones, the Aqua Julia and the Aqua Virgo. He also trained a special unit of slaves—240 in number—to repair, clean, and maintain the city's water and sanitation system. After Agrippa died in 12 B.C., Augustus appointed a water commission overseen by an official called the *curator aquarum* and his two assistants, the *audiutores*. These men inherited the slaves that Agrippa had previously trained and were able to take advantage of their experience.

the Roman Empire, besides being vulnerable to fire and river floods, Augustus so improved her appearance that he could justifiably boast: "I found Rome built of bricks; I leave her clothed in marble." . . . Among his very numerous public works three must be singled out for mention: His Forum with the Temple of Avenging Mars; the Palatine Temple of Apollo; and the Temple of Jupiter the Thunderer on the Capitoline Hill. Some of Augustus's public works were undertaken in the names of relatives, such as the colonnade [column-lined walkway] and basilica [large community hall] of his grandsons Gaius and Lucius . . . [and] the theater of his nephew Marcellus.[44]

Augustus dedicated the Theater of Marcellus, located at the southwestern base of the Capitoline hill, in 13 B.C. It sat fourteen thousand people, making it the largest theater in Rome. The structure was handsomely designed and sumptuously decorated with statues, busts, tapestries, and other finery.

Though few other buildings in Augustan Rome were as impressive as the Theater of Marcellus, one definite exception was the magnificent Ara Pacis (Altar of Peace). Viewed by many as the crowning artistic masterpiece of Augustus's reign, it was conceived as a monument to the era of peace he had initiated. Constructed of blocks of travertine (a creamy-white type of limestone) and marble, the altar was U-shaped and enclosed by marble walls sixteen feet high. Carved on the walls were bands of sculptures showing gods, goddesses, and more than a hundred human figures, including Augustus himself and his wife, Livia.

Augustus initiated many other improvements in Rome's infrastructure and layout. He passed a series of building regulations; for example, they banned the erection of houses and tenements more than seventy feet high, which reduced the number of catastrophic collapses. (Later emperors would build on his regulations by enacting even more extensive safety codes.) In addition, the Princeps made the jobs of administration and upkeep easier by dividing the city into fourteen districts, each of which consisted of several precincts. Each precinct had its administrators whom the local inhabitants elected yearly. (Augustus encouraged these elections because they gave the people the illusion that they possessed a voice in how they were governed; the truth was that these neighborhood administrators merely enacted the policies mandated by the central government, which Augustus controlled.) Finally, Augustus built or rebuilt roads, aqueducts, and sewers and created a professional firefighting force of about seven thousand men (the *vigiles*, or "watchmen").

In another vein, Augustus encouraged and supported thinkers and writers,

This reconstruction of Augustus's Theater of Marcellus, done in the 1600s, crudely attempts to capture the structure's semi-circular shape. It was the biggest theater in ancient Rome.

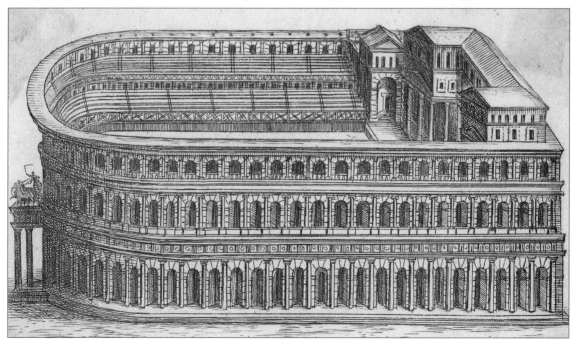

providing the impetus for what became known as the Augustan Age of Literature. "Augustus gave all possible encouragement to intellectuals," Suetonius said. "He would politely and impatiently attend readings not only of their poems and historical works, but of their speeches and dialogues."[45] The Princeps urged his wealthy friends to patronize (provide financial support for) writers and artists, giving them the luxury of exploiting their talents without having to worry about making a living. Augustus's friend Gaius Maecenas was the most prominent of these literary patrons. His literary circle of writers included Virgil, Horace, Propertius, and other noted poets. These and most of the other Augustan writers often emphasized themes that praised or promoted the "new order" Augustus had created in Rome, among them: the benefits of peace and prosperity; Rome's divine mission to rule the world; the beauties of Italy and its fields and farms; the revival of traditional Roman morality, which many believed had slipped

An idealized modern rendering of Augustus (left), attended by several wealthy literary patrons and the writers they sponsored.

Augustus Boasts of His Achievements

Octavian, renamed Augustus, was a master of political propaganda, as he showed in his public denunciations of Antony and Cleopatra during the final civil war. The first emperor also made sure to take credit for his own enormous building programs. In this passage from his Res gestae *(quoted in Lewis and Reinhold's* Sourcebook II: The Empire*), the brief summary he left of his own achievements, he brags:*

I repaired the Capitol [the Capitoline hill, on which rested temples of Jupiter] and the theater of Pompey with enormous expenditures [of money] on both works, without having my name inscribed on them. I repaired the conduits of the aqueducts [stone structures that piped water] which were falling into ruin in many places because of age. . . . I completed the Julian Forum and the basilica [meeting hall and law court] which was between the temple of Castor and the temple of Saturn, works begun . . . by my father [his adoptive father, Julius Caesar]. . . . I repaired eighty-two temples of the gods in the city . . . neglecting none which at that time required repair. . . . On my own private land I built the temple of Mars Ultor and the Augustan Forum from the spoils of war.

The Temple of Jupiter dominates the sacred Capitoline hill after the extensive restorations of Augustus's reign.

considerably in previous decades; and the glories of Rome's heroic pre–civil war past.

Augustus's Immediate Successors

Augustus's fruitful reign lasted nearly forty-five years. Finally, in August A.D. 14, while on his way to enjoy a holiday in the town of Naples, he fell ill, and his companions carried him to a nearby villa belonging to his family. "Augustus died in the same room as his father, Octavius," Suetonius later wrote. "That was 19 August, A.D. 14, at about 3 P.M. . . . In thirty-five days' time he would have attained the age of seventy-six." Suetonius added that "it was decided not to pay him excessive honors,"[46] but apparently the Roman people's depth of grief at this moment was so great that no one could resist. After his body was transported to Rome, a gigantic funeral procession carried it in a coffin topped by a couch of gold and ivory. Eventually the mourners placed the casket on a huge wooden pyre, lit it, and then released a lone eagle into the sky, symbolizing his spirit ascending into heaven. The great first-century A.D. Roman historian Tacitus offered this simple but fitting summary of the first emperor's accomplishments:

> Augustus had put the State in order not by making himself king . . . but by creating the Principate. [Under his rule] the empire's frontiers were on the ocean, or distant rivers. Armies, provinces, fleets, the whole system was interrelated [well organized and administered]. Roman citizens were protected by the law. Provincials were decently treated. Rome itself had been lavishly beautified. Force had been sparingly used—merely to preserve peace for the majority.[47]

With a few brief exceptions, this "peace for the majority" lasted for several more generations, as the Pax Romana seemed to stretch on and on. Among these exceptions were the invasion of Britain in A.D. 43 by the fourth emperor, Claudius; the suppression of a Jewish rebellion in Palestine in the late 60s; and a brief but bloody power struggle for the throne in 69. For the most part, however, Augustus's immediate successors maintained the peaceful, productive climate he had instituted, even when their personal lives were not as fulfilling or virtuous as his.

The second emperor, Tiberius—Augustus's stepson, who reigned from 14 to 37—was a case in point. At first Tiberius carried on Augustus's policies, administered the provinces efficiently, and managed the economy well. But though he had good intentions, the new ruler grew increasingly unpopular with the Roman people, partly because he did not spend much money on the gladiatorial fights and other public spectacles that they relished. He also came to delegate most of his governmental duties to a subordinate named Sejanus, who proceeded to murder and terrorize his political opponents. Meanwhile, Tiberius grew moody and withdrew from public life, finally dying a lonely old man.

The third emperor turned out to be even more antisocial than the second. Because Tiberius had no living sons, he was succeeded by Augustus's great-grandson, Gaius Caesar, who acquired the nickname of Caligula, meaning "Little Boots," as a boy. Most Romans liked the young man at first; but following a bout of serious illness, which seems to have affected his mind, he displayed increasingly twisted and corrupt behavior. According to Suetonius, he murdered

The second emperor, Tiberius, enjoys some entertainment at his retreat on the island of Capri, near the Bay of Naples. Tiberius spent his last years of life in total seclusion.

and tortured many people; he told the consuls, "I have only to give one nod and both your throats will be cut on the spot"; and bragged to his grandmother, "Bear in mind that I can treat anyone exactly as I please!"[48] Fortunately for Rome, Caligula's ministers and governors kept the administration of the realm on an even keel during his short reign (37–41), which ended with his murder by his own bodyguards.

"Absolute Power Corrupts Absolutely"

Another of Augustus's immediate successors, Nero, had an even more notorious reign (54–68) than Caligula did. And once more, the Empire was lucky that the ruler's corrupt behavior was confined mainly to his palace and the capital city and had no appreciable effect on the peace and prosperity of the post-Augustan era. The great-great-grandson of Augustus, Nero was a selfish, cruel, and extravagant individual who became a sort of poster boy for the old maxim that "absolute power corrupts absolutely." Suetonius neatly summed up Nero's reign with the observation that he "practiced every kind of obscenity." These heinous acts included personally murdering or ordering the deaths of his stepbrother,

Members of the Praetorian Guard, the emperor's personal security force, assassinate Caligula, Rome's third imperial ruler. He was succeeded by Claudius.

mother, first wife (Octavia), and numerous Roman citizens. Some of the latter were innocent bystanders whom the emperor did not even know. "As soon as night fell," Suetonius said, Nero would disguise himself and, accompanied by a few bodyguards, would "prowl the streets, . . . attack men on their way home from dinner, stab them if they offered resistance, and then drop their bodies down the sewers."[49]

Nero is perhaps most infamous for what he did after the great fire that destroyed large sections of the capital city in July 64. Many Romans came to believe that he ignited the blaze and composed songs while watching the city burn. This accusation is almost certainly untrue. But one can easily understand the source of people's suspicions. In the wake of the disaster, Nero grabbed a large area cleared by the fire and on it built a new, overly grand, and gaudy palace, the Golden House, surrounded by parklands for his own amusement. Seeing him as a pompous, wasteful despot, a number of high-placed individuals in the capital began plotting his death. And on discovering these intrigues, Nero executed and exiled hundreds of people.

Finally, it took a revolt of the army to eliminate the tyrant. Early in 68, Servius Galba, a provincial governor, was acclaimed emperor by his troops and threatened to march on Rome. When news of the rebellion reached Nero, "he fainted dead away," Suetonius recorded,

and remained mute and insensible for a long while. Coming to himself, he tore his clothes and beat his forehead. . . . [He also] formed several appalling . . . schemes for dealing with the situation. Thus, he intended to depose all army commanders . . . and execute them on the charge that they were all involved in a single conspiracy. . . . He further considered poisoning the entire Senate at a banquet; and setting fire to the city. . . . However, he had to abandon these schemes . . . because he realized their impracticability in view of the military campaign soon forced on him.[50]

A modern artist's rendition of Nero's Golden House, which was surrounded by parks and an artificial lake. His successors dismantled the structure and built the Colosseum in its place.

An Emperor Turned Mugger

According to Suetonius in this excerpt from his biography of Nero (in Lives of the Twelve Caesars), *the emperor enjoyed disguising himself and mugging innocent strangers:*

As soon as night fell, he would snatch a cap or a wig and make a round of the taverns, or prowl the streets in search of mischief—and not always innocent mischief either, because one of his games was to attack men on their way home from dinner, stab them if they offered resistance, and then drop their bodies down the sewers. He would also break into shops and rob them, afterwards opening a market at the palace with the stolen goods, . . . auctioning them himself, and squandering the proceeds. During these escapades he often risked being blinded or killed—once he was beaten almost to death by a senator whose wife he had molested, which taught him never to go out after dark unless an escort of bodyguards was following him at an unobserved distance.

Indeed, the Senate and Praetorian Guard (the emperor's personal bodyguards) suddenly recognized Galba's authority, and Nero had to flee. When some soldiers cornered him in a house, he stabbed himself in the throat and "died, with eyes glazed and bulging from their sockets, a sight which horrified everybody present."[51]

Claudius

It must be emphasized that twisted, corrupt rulers like Caligula and Nero were the exceptions that proved the rule. Most of the emperors of the Pax Romana era were capable, balanced, and fair individuals who sincerely cared about the welfare of the realm and its inhabitants. In addition, several were prolific builders whose works still stand today. Claudius, for example, who ruled from the death of Caligula in 41 to the accession of Nero in 54, constructed numerous roads and temples. However, as noted historian Chris Scarre points out:

Claudius's major building works involved engineering more than architecture. He completed two aqueducts, the Aqua Claudia, 43 miles long, and the Anio Novus, 54 miles long. . . . Claudius's most important efforts . . . were directed towards the grain supply on which the free citizenry of Rome had come to depend. . . . To alleviate shortages, Claudius undertook two huge civil engineering projects. The first of these was the draining of the Fucine Lake [southeast of Rome] to create more farmland, a project which employed 30,000 men for eleven years. . . . The second was the building of a new deep-water harbor, known as Portus, at the mouth of the Tiber near Ostia [Rome's traditional port].[52]

Claudius's efficiency and beneficence also revealed itself in less showy ways. On the one hand, he significantly expanded the civil service in the Empire's provinces. He also generously granted Roman citizenship to many provincials. These acts further strengthened the bonds of the realm's outlying regions and the central government in Italy. In addition, Claudius showed compassion for some underprivileged segments of society whose needs and sufferings were usually overlooked or neglected. He sponsored a law ensuring that orphans would be assigned proper guardians, for instance. Suetonius told of how the emperor went out of his way to help a group of mistreated slaves:

Finding that a number of sick or worn-out slaves had been marooned by their owners on the Island of Aesculapius, in the Tiber, to avoid the trouble of giving them proper medical attention, Claudius freed them all and ruled that none who

A reconstruction of the artificial harbor of Portus, the new port constructed by Claudius on the north side of the Tiber's mouth.

got well again should return to the control of his former owner; furthermore, that any owner who made away with a sick slave, rather than abandon him, should be charged with murder.[53]

This humane treatment of slaves foreshadowed other progressive social policies and laws that would be part of an emerging state welfare system in the next century.

Vespasian and Titus

One of Claudius's immediate successors was also a thoughtful ruler and great builder. Vespasian, who founded what came to be called the Flavian dynasty (family of rulers), was an honest, hardworking individual of humble background

who had risen through the army ranks to the post of general. In A.D. 68, while serving in Palestine, he received word of Nero's suicide and Galba's claim to the throne. In the next few months, Vespasian and two other powerful generals, Otho and Vitellius, claimed the throne, too. When the dust from the power struggle finally settled the following year (69, appropriately known thereafter as "the year of the four emperors"), Vespasian was firmly in control of the Empire.

Vespasian quickly demonstrated that he was a tolerant, frugal, and efficient man whose major goal was to erase the memory of Nero's misrule and restore good government to Rome. As a symbolic gesture, he ordered the distribution of coins bearing the words *Roma resurgens*, or "Rome reborn." True to this

Busts of Vespasian (left) and his eldest son, Titus, the first two of three successive emperors from the same family. Both men were able, thoughtful, and just rulers.

motto, Vespasian sponsored a burst of urban renewal that equaled or surpassed that of Claudius. According to Suetonius:

In Rome, which had been made unsightly by fires and collapsed buildings, Vespasian authorized anyone who pleased to take over the vacant sites, and build on them if the original owners failed to come forward. He personally inaugurated the restoration of the burned Capitol [the Temple of Jupiter Capitolinus, which had been badly damaged during the recent power struggle], by collecting the first basketful of rubble and carrying it away on his shoulders. . . . He also started work on several new buildings: a temple of Peace near the Forum, [and] a temple to Claudius . . . on the Caelian hill, . . . [a structure] almost completely destroyed by Nero.[54]

Vespasian's greatest and most lasting achievement was initiating construction of the Colosseum (known in his day as the Amphitheater of the Flavians, reflecting that he and his sons erected it). Completed in the heart of the capital in 81, this huge facility for the presentation of gladiatorial combats and wild animal shows sat at least fifty thousand spectators.

Following Vespasian was his eldest son, Titus, who proved to be as fair, honest, and efficient a ruler as his father. The difference was that Titus's reign (79–81) was concerned less with grand building projects (although he continued work on the Colosseum) and more with social welfare, often on a personal level. He was genuinely interested in his subjects and their problems. Often he would engage ordinary people in conversation at the public games or in the bathhouses and intently listen to their grievances. "Titus was naturally kind-hearted," Suetonius asserted.

He never took anything away from any citizen, but showed the greatest respect for private property, and would not even accept the gifts [from clients and petitioners] that were permissible and customary. . . . He also had a rule never to dismiss any petitioner without leaving him some hope that his request would be favorably considered. . . . One evening at dinner, realizing that he had done nobody any favor throughout the entire day, he spoke these memorable words: "My friends, I have wasted a day."[55]

Titus also showed how kind and concerned a ruler he was in the way he dealt with three catastrophes that struck Italy during his reign. One was the great eruption of Mount Vesuvius, in Campania, in August 79, which obliterated the nearby towns of Pompeii and Herculaneum; the second was a fire that destroyed a number of buildings in the capital; and the third was a serious disease epidemic that caused much death and suffering in Rome. "Throughout this assortment of disasters," Suetonius wrote,

This modern drawing of the destruction of Pompeii by Mount Vesuvius in A.D. 79 captures the drama and chaos of the event.

he showed far more than an emperor's concern. It resembled the deep love of a father for his children, which he conveyed . . . by helping the victims to the utmost extent of his purse. He set up a board of ex-consuls . . . to relieve distress in Campania, and . . . [established] a fund for rebuilding the stricken cities [although they turned out to be too far gone to rebuild]. . . . He stripped his own country mansions of their decorations, [and] distributed these among the public buildings and temples [that had burned in the fire]. . . . Titus attempted to cure the plague and limit its ravages by every imaginable means, human as well as divine—resorting to all sorts of sacrifices and medical remedies.[56]

Unfortunately for Rome, Titus died unexpectedly, apparently of a fever, in September 81, having ruled for a little more than two years.

"The Happiness of a Great People"

Titus's brief but beneficent reign foreshadowed the character of the second half of the Pax Romana, which proved even more stable and prosperous than the first. The highlight of the era consisted of the consecutive reigns of the emperors who ruled from 96 to 180—Nerva (96–98), Trajan (98–117), Hadrian (117–138), Antoninus Pius (138–161), and Marcus Aurelius (161–180). These men were so enlightened and productive that posterity later came to call them the "five good emperors." Under their rule, the Roman commonwealth reached its political and economic height. "If a man were called upon to fix the period in the history of the world during which the condition of the human race was most happy and prosperous," wrote the eighteenth-century English historian Edward Gibbon,

> he would without hesitation name that which elapsed from the [accession of Nerva to the death of Aurelius]. . . . Their united reigns are possibly the only period of history in which the happiness of a great people was the sole object of government. . . . The vast extent of the Roman Empire was governed by absolute power under the guidance of virtue and wisdom. The armies were restrained. . . . The forms of the civil administration were carefully preserved.[57]

Though this passage from Gibbon's great masterpiece, *The Decline and Fall of the Roman Empire*, is an exaggeration, it is not a large one. The Empire reached its greatest geographical extent under Trajan—about 3.5 million square miles,

Trajan's Column was erected to commemorate the emperor's successful conquest of Dacia (present-day eastern Hungary).

encompassing all of the lands bordering the Mediterranean, plus parts of the Near East, North Africa, and Britain. And the vast majority of people who inhabited this immense realm found it a safe, prosperous, and pleasant place to live. When he was not preoccupied with expanding the borders, Trajan devoted himself almost entirely to governing fairly and efficiently. Like Augustus and Vespasian, he was a great builder. Trajan also worked hand-in-hand with the consuls and senators in expanding the welfare system, including the establishment of special funds to help the poor. In addition, he was known for his sense of justice. His friend, the noted civil servant and letter writer Pliny the Younger, praised him, writing:

You do not sit as judge intent on enriching your privy purse [i.e., convict

Hadrian (seen in the inset over a drawing of his tomb), Trajan's successor, greatly admired Greek culture and restored numerous old buildings in Athens and other Greek cities.

Aurelius Remembers Antoninus

In his Meditations, *Marcus Aurelius, last of the so-called five good emperors, left behind his personal observations of his adoptive father, the preceding emperor Antoninus Pius. This excerpt (translated by George Long in volume 12 of* Great Books of the Western World*) paints a picture of a man who anyone in any age would be proud to have as either a father or a ruler.*

In my father I observed mildness of temper, and unchangeable resolution in the things which he had determined after due deliberation; and no vainglory [conceit] in those things which men call honors; and a love of labor and perseverance; and a readiness to listen to [others] . . . and to be satisfied on all occasions, and cheerful . . . and to be ever watchful over the things which are necessary for the administration of the Empire, and to be a good manager of the [state budget]. . . . There was in him nothing harsh nor implacable, nor violent . . . but [instead] he examined all things . . . as if he had an abundance of time, and without confusion, in an orderly way, vigorously and consistently.

Like Antoninus Pius (bottom), his adopted son and successor, Marcus Aurelius (top), was a fair, just ruler.

people of crimes with the goal of confiscating their lands, a tactic used by Nero and other emperors], and you want no reward for your decision other than to have judged rightly. Litigants stand before you concerned not for their fortunes, but for your good opinion [of them].[58]

Trajan's successor, Hadrian, was still another great builder, who erected or restored numerous structures both in Rome and the Greek city of Athens. Hadrian also further expanded the welfare system, creating free schools for poor children and strengthening laws protecting slaves from abuse. Likewise, his successors—

Antoninus Pius and Marcus Aurelius—were extraordinarily honest, ethical, and generous rulers. A Greek writer of their time, Aelius Aristides, composed a long panegyric (formal speech of praise) intended to sum up the overall achievement of Rome in the Pax Romana. He said, in part:

> The whole world speaks in unison . . . in praying this Empire may last for all time. . . . Every place is full of gymnasia, fountains, gateways, temples, shops, and schools. . . . Gifts never stop flowing from you to the cities . . . [which] shine in radiance and beauty. . . . Only those outside your Empire, if there are any, are fit to be pitied for losing such blessings. . . . Greek and [non-Greek] can now readily go wherever they please with their property or without it. . . . You have surveyed the whole world, built bridges of all sorts across rivers, cut down mountains to make paths for chariots, filled the deserts with hostels, and civilized it all with system and order.[59]

This glowing portrait, like the one Gibbon composed later, was an exaggeration; it conveniently ignored the realm's millions of slaves, who had no say in deciding their own futures, and many free but illiterate and dirt-poor farmers who knew nothing but back-breaking work from morning till night. These people, Michael Grant points out, "could scarcely be described as happy and prosperous."[60] Yet the many hymns of praise for Rome were at least inspired by one inescapable reality. Namely, despite its many faults, the Empire at its zenith was the largest, most culturally diverse, richest, most prosperous, safest, and most religiously tolerant society the world had yet seen.

Unfortunately for the inhabitants of that society, Marcus Aurelius's generation would be the last to know Rome in so admirable a state. As he sat on his throne, he and his subjects had no way of knowing that the Pax Romana was about to end. No one then living could have imagined that in the space of a mere two generations, the once seemingly invincible Roman Empire would be teetering on the brink of total collapse.

Chapter

5

Near Collapse and Rebirth: The Later Empire

Seen in historical retrospect, the Roman realm had undergone several major transformations. One had been the replacement of the Monarchy with the Republic; soon afterward the small Roman city-state had rapidly expanded into an empire encompassing many nations and peoples; next, the republican government had collapsed and given way to the autocratic Principate, which had flourished, along with the Roman economy and people, during the productive years of the Pax Romana.

Now, the reign of the sixteenth emperor, Marcus Aurelius, witnessed the initial stirrings of a new transformation for the Roman world. His immediate successors faced increasingly serious in-

ternal and external problems. And a mere half century after his death in A.D. 180, the Empire plunged into a crisis even more severe than the series of civil wars that had wrecked the Republic in the days of Cicero, Caesar, and Octavian. In what historians sometimes refer to as the Anarchy, any remnants of the Pax Romana's peace and economic stability were shattered.[61] Large Germanic tribes invaded the realm's northern borders, while in the East, Roman provinces faced attacks by the Sassanian Persian Empire (centered in what are now Iran and Iraq). At the same time, Rome was plagued by political instability; poor leadership; a breakdown of military discipline and law and order; a serious decline in farming and trade; a crippling devaluation of money; and the spread of gut-wrenching poverty, misery, fear, and uncertainty.

Never before had Rome had to deal with so many debilitating internal and external threats at one time. Unable to cope, in the mid-third century the Empire fragmented, imploded, and was almost destroyed. Yet the Roman people showed that they still possessed some core remnants of that stubborn courage and resiliency that had allowed them to bounce back from the brink of doom so many times in the past. In the late third

A sketch of the equestrian statue of Marcus Aurelius. Shortly after his death, Rome entered a period of political chaos known as the Anarchy.

century, a new Roman realm rose from the rubble of the Anarchy; modern historians often call it the Later Empire. Rome was now a grimmer, less hopeful place than it had been in the days when the average Roman took for granted that his country was invincible and destined to rule the world forever. Having barely escaped complete destruction in recent years, the inhabitants of the Later Empire had few or no such naïve and romantic illusions.

The Leadership in Decline

The Anarchy that eventually led to the Later Empire did not materialize suddenly or without warning. In fact, most of the problems Rome faced in the great crisis of the third century began on a smaller scale in the latter years of the second century. During Marcus Aurelius's reign, for instance, bands of Germanic tribesmen crossed the Danube River, which had long marked the northern border of the Roman realm, and raided several Roman provinces. The emperor drove these intruders back, an endeavor that required the better part of his reign. But these heroic efforts proved little more than temporary stopgap measures in the long run. Among the Celts of northern Europe, whom the Greeks and Romans referred to as "barbarians," populations were growing and unrest was increasing. In the years to come, the Empire would have to fight these invaders again and again. As historian Anthony Kamm puts it, "As soon as one . . . invasion [was] averted, another would break out or threaten in a different part of the Empire."[62]

Unfortunately for Rome, it faced this growing external threat at a time when the quality of Roman leadership was rapidly decreasing. Marcus Aurelius's son, Commodus, who came to power on his father's death, was, like Caligula and Nero before him, a self-centered individual with little concept of efficient or fair government. Commodus squandered large sums of money from the public treasury. He also initiated a reign of terror in the capital, ordering the executions of many people for minor offenses. In addition, he reversed his father's foreign policy of pushing back the barbarians by permitting groups of these former invaders to settle in some of the border provinces.

Commodus died by assassination in 192. There then followed a long and bloody power struggle in which a number of army generals in various parts of the Empire claimed the throne. The winner of this contest, Septimius Severus, who had full control of the Empire from 197 to 211, was a strong military tactician who maintained a powerful,

The cruel and corrupt Commodus is strangled to death by Narcissus, a champion wrestler.

well-disciplined army and largely kept the Germanic tribes at bay. However, he had no talent for domestic affairs and did nothing to halt the realm's steadily worsening internal problems. The economy was growing weaker, partly from a general decline in farming and trade, but more so from a devaluation of money caused by minting coins with cheap metal alloys instead of silver. Severus just made things worse by further decreasing the amount of silver in coins. He also raised

Commodus's Disreputable Character

In this excerpt from the Augustan History, *an unknown fourth-century chronicler captures Commodus's disreputable character:*

He would drink till dawn and squander the resources of the Roman Empire. In the evening he flitted through the taverns to the brothels [houses of prostitution]. He sent to rule the provinces persons who were either his allies in crime or had been recommended by criminals. He became so hated by the Senate that he was filled with a savage passion to destroy that great order. . . . Commodus . . . killed his sister Lucilla. . . . Then, having debauched [seduced] his other sisters . . . he even gave one of the concubines [mistresses] the name of his mother. His wife, whom he had caught in adultery, he drove out, then banished her, and subsequently killed her.

taxes to pay for his military spending, which placed a heavy financial burden on the Roman people. His lack of true concern for his subjects comes though strongly in the advice he offered his sons, Caracalla and Geta, on his deathbed: "Agree with each other, give money to the soldiers, and scorn all other men."[63]

The quality of the administrative and moral leadership of Rome's government declined still further under the brutal Caracalla (reigned 211–217). Ignoring his father's advice about getting along with his brother, he murdered Geta after the two had ruled jointly for only ten months. Like Severus, Caracalla was popular with the soldiers but largely ignored the needs of his people. It is true that in 212 the new emperor granted citizenship to all free inhabitants of the realm, but as Chris Scarre points out, this move was not motivated by generosity. Instead, "the intention was most likely to widen the obligation for public service and increase imperial revenues, since citizens were liable to pay additional taxes."[64]

War, Turmoil, and Fear

One of Caracalla's own officers killed him in 217, after which the throne was occupied by a series of short-lived and ineffective leaders—Macrinus (217–218), Elagabalus (218–222), and Severus Alexander (222–235). During their reigns, the economy continued to disintegrate and the realm grew increasingly unstable. The roughly fifty years of the Anarchy now ensued, during which more than fifty rulers claimed to be emperor. About half of them received formal acknowledgment in that role; however, no more than eighteen possessed any real legitimacy. The chaotic and dangerous atmosphere in which they operated is revealed by two grim statistics: An average reign in the period lasted just two and a half years; and all but one of these rulers died by assassination or other violent means.

All the men who sat on the throne in these turbulent years faced a host of serious problems that were virtually unknown in the Pax Romana period. Trade continued to decline, while poverty and crime reached alarming levels. Meanwhile, the coinage was practically worthless, and the soldiers made up for their lack of pay by looting Roman as well as enemy villages and farms.

As bad as these internal problems were, they were often largely ignored by the government because the external threat of foreign invaders generally dominated the era and most preoccupied the soldier-emperors. The first wave of intruders were German peoples who assaulted the Danube frontier in the 230s. One major group, the Goths, who inhabited the lands north of the Black Sea, raided Rome's northern border provinces in 238 and in 251 defeated and killed the emperor Decius (reigned 249–251). In time the Goths split into two groups—the Ostrogoths and Visigoths, both of whom remained a threat to the Empire. In the meantime, other northern European peoples and tribes threatened to overrun some of Rome's most important regions. In 260 the Alamanni penetrated

Septimius Severus (left) and his son, Caracalla. Caracalla killed his brother and co-emperor, Geta, but was later murdered by an army officer, Macrinus.

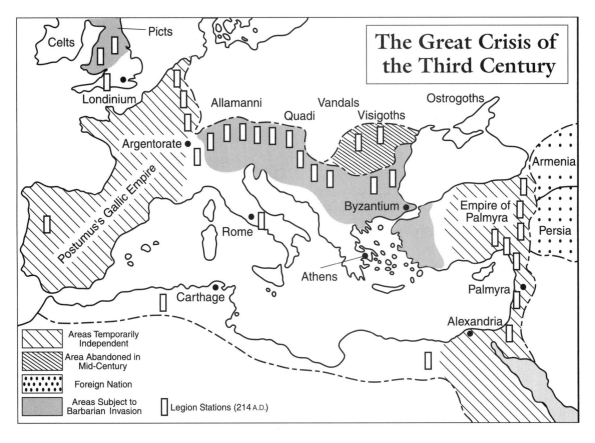

The Great Crisis of the Third Century

Celts
Picts
Londinium
Allamanni
Quadi
Vandals
Visigoths
Ostrogoths
Argentorate
Postumus's Gallic Empire
Armenia
Byzantium
Empire of Palmyra
Persia
Rome
Athens
Palmyra
Carthage
Alexandria

Areas Temporarily Independent
Area Abandoned in Mid-Century
Foreign Nation
Areas Subject to Barbarian Invasion
Legion Stations (214 A.D.)

northern Italy, and other tribes invaded Gaul and Spain.

The western and northern borders were not the only ones under attack. In 253 the Sassanian Persians captured one of Rome's largest and most prosperous cities—Antioch, in Syria. Rising to the challenge, the emperor Valerian (reigned 253–260) held the Sassanians at bay for a while; but in 260 he was captured during a negotiations session. The Persians then stepped up their attacks on Rome's eastern provinces. (Valerian remained a prisoner for his few remaining years, and when he died, the Sassanian king ordered him skinned and his hide hung up in a Persian temple.)

The almost constant war, turmoil, fear, and uncertainty of these years were bound to take a toll on the Roman populace. Trade almost ceased entirely, and outbreaks of famine and disease became common. Making matters worse, groups of Roman soldiers took advantage of the beleaguered populace by stealing and raping at will. A contemporary writer, Herodian, penned this account of imperial troops pillaging and a frightened population in the northern Italian city of Aquileia in 238:

A large population lived there. . . . At this time, however, the population was even further increased by all the crowds streaming thither from the countryside, leaving the neighboring towns and villages to seek safety inside the great city and its surrounding walls. . . . Finding the houses of the suburbs deserted, [the marauding soldiers] cut down all the vines and trees, set some on fire, and made a shambles of the once-thriving countryside. . . . After destroying all this to the root, the army pressed on to the walls . . . and strove to demolish at least some part of the walls, so that they might break in and sack everything, razing the city and leaving the land a deserted pasturage.[65]

Diocletian and the Tetrarchy

The ruin of Aquileia was no isolated incident, but part of an overall breakdown of law and order that went hand-in-hand with the foreign invasions, poverty, and other horrors of the day. The resplendent and seemingly invincible realm praised so highly by Aristides and other panegyrists only a century before was now in a state of chaos and near collapse. "It seemed," Michael Grant remarks, "as if the Roman world, which was . . . split into fragments . . . could not possibly survive." Yet incredibly, the Romans once more managed to stave off annihilation in the eleventh

Men Accustomed to the Hardships of War

The fourth-century Roman historian Aurelius Victor penned this brief description (quoted in Naphtali Lewis and Meyer Reinhold's Roman Civilization, Sourcebook II: The Empire*) of the character of the men appointed by Diocletian to the Tetrarchy:*

All these men were, indeed, natives of Illyria [the region that became Yugoslavia in modern times]; but although little cultured, they were of great service to the state, because they were inured [accustomed] to the hardships of rural life and of war. . . . The harmony which prevailed among them proved above all that their native ability and their skill in military science, which they had acquired from [the strong soldier-emperors] Aurelian and Probus, almost sufficed to compensate for lack of high character. Finally, they looked up to Diocletian as to a father or as one would to a mighty god.

hour. Starting in the year 268, a series of tough and capable soldier-emperors emerged and, Grant continues, "in one of the most striking reversals in world history, Rome's foes were hurled back."[66]

In this sculpture, Diocletian and his three fellow tetrarchs embrace, signifying their dedication to joint rule over the vast territories controlled by Rome.

The culmination of this great reversal of fortunes for the Roman nation was the accession of the most talented and successful of the new breed of strong military emperors. In 284 Diocletian, the leader of the imperial household cavalry, was acclaimed emperor by the army. Hailing from Spalato (or Split), in the province of Dalmatia (on the Adriatic Sea's eastern coast), he was of humble origins and had risen through the ranks through talent and hard work. He ruled for more than twenty years, the longest imperial reign since that of Antoninus Pius more than a century before; and in that highly productive span, he gave what had seemed like a doomed realm a transfusion of sound government that allowed it to enjoy another century of vigorous life.

To ensure that he would not be killed before he could effect major reforms, as well as to restore the prestige the throne had largely lost in recent years, Diocletian transformed the Roman court into an absolute monarchy resembling that of Sassanian Persia. First, he dropped all pretense of the emperor being the Princeps, a man of the people. Instead, he assumed the title of *dominus* (lord) and ordered that anyone approaching must bow low and kiss his robe. He also filled the Roman court with elaborate ceremony and layers of guards and spies, creating an air of awe and superstition that discouraged open dissent and assassination plots.

This proved only the tip of the iceberg, so to speak, of Diocletian's reforms.

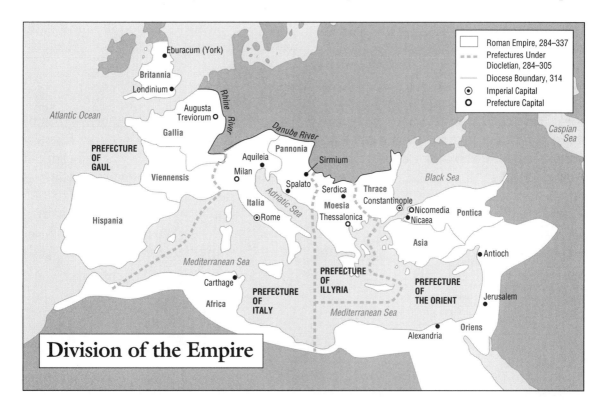

Division of the Empire

Some were of an administrative nature, designed to make ruling so large and diverse an empire more efficient, as well as to strengthen the authority of the central government. "Frontier provinces were divided into smaller units," noted scholars Arthur Boak and William Sinnigen explain,

largely in order to provide closer supervision of border garrisons and weaken the power of the commanders. The provinces were grouped into new administrative districts called *dioceses*. These changes greatly increased the number of civilian and military personnel in the service of

the state. Mistrustful of his own bureaucracy, Diocletian reorganized the imperial secret service . . . and used it to inform on governmental operations.[67]

Even with these changes, Diocletian realized, it would not be easy for a single person to administer the huge Roman commonwealth. A practical individual, he faced the reality that he must delegate authority; and accordingly, in March 286 he appointed a trusted lieutenant named Maximian as his "Caesar," second in command and heir to the throne. A few months later, Diocletian granted Maximian the title of "Augustus," making him co-emperor, although a subordinate one. Diocletian, who remained the primary ruler, held court in the eastern city of Nicomedia (in northern Asia Minor). Maximian administered the western sector of the realm from Rome. A few years later, Diocletian further divided the leadership. He and Maximian chose Caesars of their own, so that the Empire was now ruled by a four-man combination—the Tetrarchy, touted by a late Roman writer as "four rulers of the world . . . brave, wise, kind, generous, respectful to the Senate, friends of the people, moderate, revered, devoted, pious."[68]

Attempted Economic Reforms

Diocletian also made a valiant effort to reform the Empire's economy, which lay in shambles as a result of the widespread corruption, abuse, and neglect of the Anarchy. First he tried to stabilize the money supply by issuing pure gold and silver coins. This seemed to make sense, since debasing the coinage with cheap al-

Diocletian's Edict on Prices

Excerpted here is the introductory section of Diocletian's famous economic edict of 301 (quoted in Lewis and Reinhold's Sourcebook II: The Empire*), an attempt to shore up Rome's economy by imposing maximum prices that people could charge for goods and services.*

We . . . by the gracious favor of the gods . . . must surround the peace which we established for eternity with the necessary defenses of justice. If the excesses perpetrated by persons of unlimited and frenzied avarice [greed] could be checked by some self-restraint . . . the situation could perhaps be faced with . . . silence [inaction]. . . . But the only desire of these uncontrolled madmen is to have no thought for the common need. . . . Therefore, we, who are the protectors of the human race, are agreed, as we view the situation, that decisive legislation is necessary, so that the long-hoped-for solutions which mankind itself could not provide may . . . be [applied] for the general betterment of all. . . . We hasten, therefore, to apply the remedies long demanded by the [crippling economic] situation, satisfied that no one can complain. . . . Aroused justly and rightfully by all the facts which are detailed above, and in response to the needs of mankind itself, which appears to be praying for release [from economic misery], we have decided that maximum prices of articles for sale must be established.

loys had been one of the root causes of the realm's financial troubles. However, the effort was not successful, mainly because gold and silver remained in short supply. So the government continued to pay salaries to soldiers and civil servants in coins of limited value.

One consequence of using devalued money was that prices of goods kept going up and people had trouble making ends meet. With this in mind, Diocletian attempted to regulate prices, based on the theory that this would reduce inflation and eventually increase the buying power of money. In 301 he issued a major economic edict, saying: "We have decided that maximum prices of articles for sale must be established. . . . Thus, when the pressure of high prices appears anywhere—may the gods avert such a calamity!—avarice [greed] . . . will be checked by the limits fixed in our statute."[69] The edict was accompanied by a long list of prices set by the emperor and his advisers. Henceforth a pair of women's boots could cost no more than 60 *denarii* per pair, pork (the Romans' favorite meat) could not exceed 12 *denarii* a pound, and a teacher of arithmetic could charge up to but not more than 75 *denarii* a day. This effort to cap prices was well meaning. But it ultimately failed, mainly because people did not like the government telling them what they could earn or charge for goods. In general, most Romans either ignored the new rules or found ways to get around them.

Diocletian's ineffective regulation of prices was only part of his economic plan.

Another part—an empirewide census—had more lasting effects on the realm. A major purpose of the census was to interview people to determine the worth of land, farm animals, and other property throughout the realm. This was important because a large proportion of the taxes people paid were in the form of goods such as livestock, jewelry, and food—a kind of payment called indiction. The problem was that the government collected these goods in a spotty, inequitable manner and had no idea of how much it might acquire in any given year. Obviously, this made it extremely difficult, if not impossible, for the country's leaders to plan ahead. Diocletian's regional censuses, which his successors kept in force, created a more efficient tax system (at least for the moment) and aided government planners.

The Rise of Constantine

Though not all of Diocletian's reforms were successful, he imposed enough positive change to restore a good deal of the security and order lost during the Anarchy. In retrospect, it is clear that this made possible the development of an even more sweeping change in the course of Roman civilization—the rise of Christianity to a controlling position in the government. Though this momentous turn of events was a complex process that took close to four generations to complete, it would not have been possible without the deeds and influence of one of Diocletian's leading successors, Constantine I.

Indeed, the Christian movement had already existed for nearly three centuries but had remained small and marginal, mainly because many Romans were suspicious of Christianity. In their view, Christians were antisocial because they often kept to themselves; seemed intolerant of other gods and faiths; refused to worship the emperor; and were widely seen as a potential threat to public order. The result was that the Roman government periodically persecuted the Christians and kept them from gaining widespread acceptance in society. By contrast, under

Constantine and his troops are amazed by the sight of a glowing cross over the sun. Constantine became convinced that it was a favorable omen sent by the Christian god.

Constantine, who befriended them, they were able to begin shedding the negative stereotypes they had long borne. And in the decades following his reign, they acquired both social acceptance and major political power.

Constantine's rise, which was to prove so crucial to Christianity's triumph, began shortly after Diocletian retired from his imperial office in 305 (an unprecedented move in Roman politics). Before leaving, Diocletian created a new Tetrarchy that he hoped would continue his reforms and maintain peace throughout the realm. But he was disappointed when the men who made up that ruling alliance rapidly fell into mutual discord and a years-long power struggle ensued. Among the claimants to the throne was Constantine. In 312 he marched on Rome, which had recently been seized illegally by Maxentius, son of Diocletian's original co-emperor, Maximian. At the city's Milvian Bridge, the opposing armies clashed and Constantine was victorious.

More important than the battle itself in the long run was the fact that Constantine's soldiers had gone into the fight with a Christian emblem painted on their shields. (It was a combination of the first two letters of Christos, the Greek version of Christ's name.) As a young man, Constantine had come to know and trust a number of Christians and had gladly accepted the support of their god, along with that of traditional Roman deities, in his efforts to gain power. The Christian bishop Eusebius, who knew Constantine

personally, later claimed that the day before the battle at the bridge, a glowing cross had appeared in the sky near the sun. "At this sight" said Eusebius, Constantine "was struck with amazement, and his whole army also." That night, the story went, Jesus Christ came to Constantine in a dream and commanded him thereafter to use a Christian symbol "as a safeguard in all engagements with his enemies."[70]

The truth of this tale is uncertain. But the evidence suggests that, for whatever reason, Constantine did attribute his victory over Maxentius to the Christian god; and, following custom, he felt obliged to repay the deity by helping its adherents. This did not mean that Constantine thought the Christian god was better or more powerful than the other gods he still accepted. Indeed, he did not convert to the faith at this moment, but simply treated it as a legitimate and worthy religion, a status it had never enjoyed before.

Christ Above the Caesars

After the battle at the Milvian Bridge, Constantine emerged as undisputed master of the western part of the Roman Empire. However, other powerful Romans were still disputing control of the eastern part, among them Maximinus Daia and Valerius Licinius. Constantine soon decided it was to his advantage to back Licinius. The two met at Milan in February 313, and each agreed to recognize the other's dominance in his respective sphere of the realm. They also issued

Constantine as a Religious Mediator

Constantine arbitrated several disputes among the Christian bishops. The first occurred in 313, when Donatus, bishop of Numidia, asked the emperor not to allow a priest named Caecilian to become a bishop. Donatus and his followers, who became known as the Donatists, pointed out that during a recent Christian persecution some church leaders had handed over the Scriptures to be burned. This, the Donatists argued, was an immoral and criminal act. Furthermore, the clergyman who was scheduled to make Caecilian a bishop was one of these criminals, so the ceremony would not be valid. However, the bishop of Rome disagreed with this view and condemned the Donatists. In 316 Constantine sided with the bishop and ordered that the Donatists be thrown out of their churches.

Constantine also became involved in a controversy known as the Arian heresy, after Arius, a priest of Alexandria, Egypt. Arius claimed that Jesus Christ was not God; in fact, he said, this was impossible because Jesus was changeable and therefore imperfect, whereas God was unchangeable and perfect. When a huge argument erupted among the bishops over this issue, Constantine called a great council in 325 at Nicaea (in Asia Minor), the first of the seven Ecumenical Councils held by the early church. The emperor agreed with the majority, which opposed the Arians. It appears that he urged the churchmen to accept the idea of *homoousios*, "of the same substance," basically suggesting that Christ and God were one and the same being.

In this seventeenth-century depiction, Constantine convenes the Christian bishops at Nicaea in 325.

the so-called Edict of Milan, a decree that granted toleration to Christians all over the Empire.[71] "When under happy auspices," the document began,

> I, Constantine Augustus, and I, Licinius Augustus, had come to Milan and held an inquiry about all matters such as pertain to the common advantage and good. . . . We resolved to issue decrees by which esteem and reverence for the Deity might be procured, that is, that we might give all Christians freedom of choice to follow the ritual which they wished.[72]

It appears that Licinius considered the edict an expedient political move that could be undone as easily as it was done. About three years later, he launched an anti-Christian persecution, violating the decree and angering Constantine, who was more serious in his support of the Christians. At any rate, by this time arguments over the succession and territorial borders had all but shredded the treaty between the two men. They fought a civil war that ended with an overwhelming victory by Constantine in July 324 at Adrianople, in northern Greece. That left Constantine as sole emperor, the first ruler to control both parts of the realm since Diocletian had begun to share leadership in the 280s.

Constantine continued to support the Christians in the last years of his reign. In his role as Rome's overall spiritual leader (one held by all emperors since the days of Augustus), he mediated a number of contentious disputes among the bishops. He also did the faith another important service by founding Constantinople, "the city of Constantine," in May 330 on the site of the Greek town of Byzantium (on the shores of the strait leading into the Black Sea). Probably his main goal at the time was to establish a strong base from which to defend the Empire's eastern sphere against attacks from the north and east. But as a result of the increasing power and influence of Christianity, the city grew into a great Christian stronghold.

In the spring of 337, Constantine fell ill and died. In his final moments, he received baptism and officially converted to Christianity, giving the faith another enormous boost. His three sons—Constantine II (reigned 337–340), Constans (337–350), and Constantius II (337–361)—were all Christian rulers who expanded the powers and privileges of Christian clergymen and rendered bishops immune from prosecution by secular (nonchurch) courts. After that, all Roman emperors, save one (Julian, sole ruler from 361 to 363), were Christians.

Now, emboldened by support from the highest levels, zealous Christian bishops increasingly openly attacked pagan symbols, beliefs, and practices. Most influential of all was Ambrose, bishop of Milan, who got the emperor Gratian (reigned 367–383) to relinquish the office of chief priest of the state religion and to seize the funds of the state priests.

The influential bishop Ambrose (with the white beard) asserts his moral authority over the emperor Theodosius I by stopping him from attending church services.

Also at Ambrose's urging, the emperor Theodosius I (379–395) closed the traditional pagan temples, demolishing some and turning others into museums. This included a ban on all non-Christian cults, sacrifices, and ceremonies across the whole Empire, which meant a shutdown of the famous Greek oracle at Delphi and another Greek-based institution, the Olympic Games, which were dedicated to Zeus (the Roman Jupiter). As Robert Kebric puts it, while Theodosius was "orchestrating the final realization of a Christian Roman Empire," Ambrose and other leading Christians "were already setting the foundation for the Medieval Church. The door was fast closing on the ancient world."[73] Indeed, though no one knew it at the time, Rome's days were definitely numbered; even as Ambrose, Theodosius, and their supporters were busy raising Christ above the Caesars, the peoples of northern Europe were again on the move and threatening Rome's frontiers. This time there would be no stopping them.

Rome's Decline and Disintegration

"The fall of the Western Roman Empire was one of the most significant transformations throughout the whole of human history," writes Michael Grant.

> A hundred years before it happened, Rome was an immense power, defended by an immense army. A hundred years later, power and army had vanished. There was no longer any Western Empire at all. Its territory was occupied by a group of German kingdoms.[74]

How could such a tremendous downfall have occurred? How is it that a realm as powerful, long-lived, and resilient as Rome disintegrated in little more than a century?

These questions have consistently haunted the Western world during the roughly fifteen centuries that have elapsed since Rome's demise. And literally thousands of books and articles have discussed and tried to explain this seminal event. The most famous of these, which is still seen as the classic work in the genre, is *The Decline and Fall of the Roman Empire*, published a volume at a time by Edward Gibbon between 1776 and 1788. Gibbon held that the Roman state became so large and complex that it could no longer govern itself efficiently. He also cited the negative influence of Christianity, whose pacifist ideas deteriorated Rome's old martial spirit, leaving it open to predators. Those predators, he said, were the less cultured peoples of

Rome's Primitive Means of Production

One of the reasons that Rome declined was that its means of sustaining the production of food, clothes, and other essentials was backward and precarious. It was therefore at risk during chaotic conditions like those caused by the barbarian invasions. This astute analysis is by the late, great classical historian A.H.M. Jones (from his masterful Constantine and the Conversion of Europe*).*

There were coming to be more idle mouths than the primitive economic system of the Roman Empire could feed. It is hard to remember that, despite its great achievements in law and administration, the splendid architecture of its cities and the luxurious standard of living of its aristocracy, the Roman Empire was, in its methods of production, in some ways more primitive than the early Middle Ages. Agriculture followed a wasteful two-field system of alternate crop and fallow. Yarn was spun by hand with a spindle, and textiles laboriously woven on clumsy hand looms. Even corn was ground in hand querns or at best mills turned by oxen. Windmills had not been invented and watermills were still rare. In these circumstances the feeding and clothing of an individual demanded a vast expenditure of human labor, and the maintenance of any substantial number of economically unproductive persons laid a heavy burden on the rest.

central and northern Europe. "The endless column of barbarians pressed on the Roman Empire with accumulated weight," he writes. "And if the foremost were destroyed, the vacant space was instantly replenished by new assailants."[75]

Today the vast majority of historians agree that the barbarian invasions of the late fourth century and most of the fifth century constituted one of the two major causes of Rome's fall. The other main cause, they suggest, was of an internal rather than external nature. The Empire perished, Grant states, "because of certain internal flaws which prevented resolute resistance to the invaders."[76] Chief among these flaws was the decline of the once-mighty Roman army. At the very same time that Rome faced the worst threat ever to its borders, the Empire's military establishment grew increasingly weak, less disciplined, and ineffective. This made the final collapse inevitable.

The Huns, the Visigoths, and Adrianople

In examining these dire external and internal problems and how they determined the events of the Roman Empire's last century of existence, a logical place to begin is 378. This is the year of a major Roman defeat that, in retrospect, marked the beginning of the Empire's century-long final decline.

By this fateful date, the separation of the realm into two sections, a process Diocletian and Constantine had initiated, was becoming increasingly pronounced. On the western throne sat the sons of Valentinian I—Gratian and Valentinian II, both weak emperors. In charge in the East was their uncle, Valens, who also lacked strength as a ruler. These men and their advisers had no inkling of the immense pressures building among the Germanic tribes to the north. Indeed, Gibbon points out:

> The Romans were ignorant of the extent of their danger, and the number of their enemies. Beyond the Rhine and Danube [Rivers], the northern countries of Europe . . . were filled with innumerable tribes of hunters and shepherds, poor, voracious [hungry], and turbulent; bold in arms and impatient to ravish the fruits of industry.[77]

All that was needed to set these restless tribes in motion was a strong push from some quarter.

That push was quite unexpectedly provided by the Huns, a fierce nomadic people from central Asia. The fourth-century Roman historian Ammianus Marcellinus described them as "abnormally savage," with "squat bodies, strong limbs, and thick necks." Moreover, he wrote:

The Huns sweep across Europe, driving the Germans and other tribal peoples into Rome's northern border provinces.

Their way of life is so rough that they have no use for fire or seasoned food, but live on the roots of wild plants and the half-raw flesh of any sort of animals, which they warm a little by placing it between their thighs and the backs of their horses. . . . Once they have put their necks into some dingy shirt they never take it off or change it till it rots and falls to pieces. . . . When they join battle they advance in packs, uttering their various war-cries. Being lightly equipped and very sudden in their movements they can deliberately scatter and gallop about at random, inflicting tremendous slaughter.[78]

A few years before Gratian and Valentinian II ascended the western throne,

---

The Slaughter at Adrianople

In this gripping excerpt from his History, *the fourth-century historian Ammianus Marcellinus describes the disastrous Roman defeat at Adrianople in 378.*

Amid the clashing of arms and weapons on every side . . . sounding the death-knell of the Roman cause, our retreating troops rallied with shouts of mutual encouragement. But, as the fighting spread like fire and numbers of them were transfixed by arrows and whirling javelins, they lost heart. Then the opposing lines came into collision like ships of war and pushed each other to and fro, heaving under the reciprocal motion like the waves of the sea. Our left wing penetrated as far as the very wagons [of the enemy camp] . . . but it was abandoned by the rest of the cavalry, and under pressure of numbers gave way and collapsed like a broken dike. This left the infantry unprotected and so closely huddled together that a man could hardly wield his sword or draw back his arm once he had stretched it out. Dust rose in such clouds as to hide the sky, which rang with frightful shouts. . . . The barbarians poured on in huge columns, trampling down horse and man and crushing our ranks so as to make an orderly retreat impossible. Our men were too close-packed to have any hope of escape; so they resolved to die like heroes, faced the enemy's swords, and struck back at their assailants. . . . In this mutual slaughter so many were laid low that the field was covered with the bodies of the slain, while the groans of the dying and severely wounded filled all who heard them with abject fear.

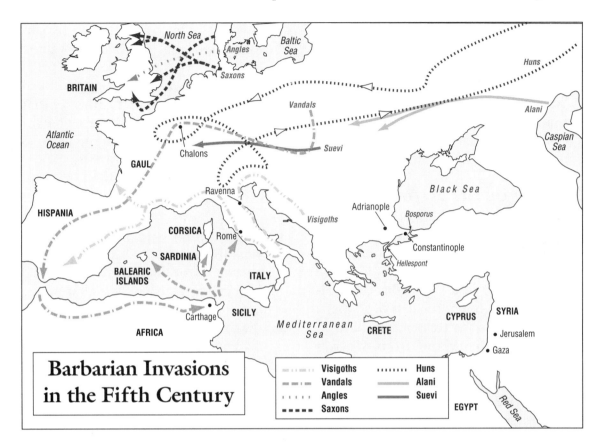

Barbarian Invasions in the Fifth Century

⋯⋯ Visigoths		⋯⋯⋯ Huns	
— ▪ — Vandals		▬▬▬ Alani	
⋯⋯ Angles		▬▬▬ Suevi	
▬ ▬ ▬ Saxons			

the Huns swept into eastern Europe, setting in motion a series of tremendous migrations of tribal peoples. Some sought to escape the frightening Huns; other groups situated farther west found their own territories swamped by the escapees. Franks, Goths, Vandals, Angles, and numerous others were forced to move, and many of them spread into Rome's northern provinces. Members of one tribe, the Visigoths, crossed the Danube into Thrace in large numbers. And Valens reacted by permitting them to settle there, probably anticipating that he could recruit many of their men for his army.

The deal went sour, however, when the emperor's agents tried to exploit the Visigoths. In retaliation, they began plundering the countryside, and Valens had no choice but to use force to stop them. His next mistake was failing to wait for Gratian to arrive from the West with more troops. The impatient Valens attacked the Visigoths on his own near Adrianople, in eastern Thrace, on August 9, 378, and ended up dying along with forty thousand of his soldiers. According to Ammianus:

As the fighting spread like fire and numbers of [Romans] were transfixed by arrows and whirling javelins, they lost heart. . . . Dust rose in such clouds as to hide the sky, which rang with frightful shouts. . . . The barbarians poured on in huge columns, trampling down horse and man and crushing our ranks so as to make an orderly retreat impossible.[79]

Decline of the Army

The crippling defeat at Adrianople came at a very bad time for the Romans. On the one hand, the barbarian invasions were just beginning and would grow larger in scope in the decades that followed. On the other, the loss of so many troops at once was a tremendous blow to the Roman military, one from which it never fully recovered. Many of the forty thousand dead were never replaced, and those replacements that did materialize often proved less disciplined, less well trained, and less reliable than the soldiers of past eras. This was the beginning of a steady deterioration of the Roman army, which would become a crucial factor in the Empire's decline and fall.

A number of problems contributed to this overall military decline. Because the government experienced increasing financial troubles, it could not afford to pay the soldiers very much. Just as frustrating, wages often went unpaid for months or even years, which proved to be very bad for military morale. Lack of funding also caused the quality of weapons and armor to decline. And recruiting new troops was more and more

difficult, partly because some Christians refused to fight, but also because joining the army was no longer seen as a worthwhile, patriotic endeavor, as it had been in earlier centuries. The result was that many young men used whatever means necessary to avoid service; some went so far as to cut off their own thumbs. (When this practice became common, Roman leaders imposed the death penalty, but later, when they were more desperate for new recruits, they forced such amputees to serve in spite of their disfigurement.)

Another factor that contributed to the ongoing military decline was that native Romans were gradually replaced in the ranks with Germans and other barbarians. This had happened on an occasional basis and very small scale in prior centuries. But the process became much larger in scale and an increasing problem after Gratian appointed a tough army general named Theodosius to succeed the slain Valens on the eastern throne. In 382 Theodosius brokered a deal with the Visigoths, victors of the battle of Adrianople. He allowed them to settle in Thrace permanently in return for supplying recruits for the Roman army. Other similar deals were struck by Theodosius and succeeding emperors with various tribes, whose warriors became a larger and larger component of the Roman army. Modern scholars often call this process the "barbarization" of the Roman military. It did not take long for it to start taking a toll in the ranks, especially in a loss of discipline, long one of the strongest traits of Roman soldiers. Theo-

The eastern emperor Theodosius (right) meets with Visogothic leaders prior to the outbreak of hostilities between the Romans and Visigoths. Valens was later defeated and killed by the Visigoths.

dosius's barbarian "allies," historian Arther Ferrill points out,

> began immediately to demand great rewards for their service and to show an independence that in drill, discipline and organization meant catastrophe. They fought under their own native commanders, and the barbaric system of discipline was in no way as severe as the Roman. Eventually Roman soldiers saw no reason to do what barbarian troops in Roman service were rewarded heavily for not doing. . . . Too long and too close association with barbarian warriors, as allies in the Roman army, had ruined the qualities that made Roman armies great. . . . [By A.D. 440] the Roman army in

the West had become little more than a barbarian army itself.[80]

A Steady Loss of Territory

At the same time that barbarian warriors were joining the ranks of the Roman army, their leaders were negotiating with the Roman government and concluding deals that would ultimately prove disastrous for the Empire. Theodosius exempted the Visigoths from normal taxation, for example, passing up the opportunity to bring needed revenue into the treasury. Even worse, he agreed to accord them the status of "federates," essentially equal allies living within their own little parcel of the Empire. This set an ominous precedent for the future because the Visigoths, not the central Roman government, now controlled that parcel; for the first time in history, a section of the Roman realm was no longer under the direct jurisdiction of the government. Under Theodosius's successors, one foreign group after another gained federate status in the western provinces. This

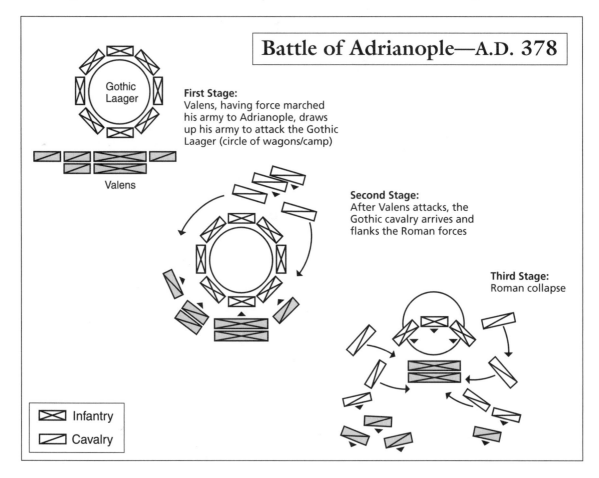

Battle of Adrianople—A.D. 378

Gothic Laager

First Stage:
Valens, having force marched his army to Adrianople, draws up his army to attack the Gothic Laager (circle of wagons/camp)

Valens

Second Stage:
After Valens attacks, the Gothic cavalry arrives and flanks the Roman forces

Third Stage:
Roman collapse

Infantry
Cavalry

steadily weakened the western Roman government, which lost more and more territory.

The imperial government faced other problems as well in the late fourth and early fifth centuries. Various claimants to the throne, most of them illegal, emerged on a periodic basis and fomented rebellions, which the legitimate emperors had to put down at great cost in money and soldiers. Meanwhile, new barbarian groups regularly threatened the northern borders. Dealing with these and other problems not only drained the state treasury, but also demanded strong central leadership, which was in increasingly short supply.

Theodosius was the last really strong ruler in the West. He was also the last emperor to rule over both the eastern and western Roman spheres. When he passed away in 395, his eleven-year-old son, Honorius, succeeded him in the West, while his other son, Arcadius, aged seventeen, took the eastern throne. At a time when a united realm was needed to defend against foreign intruders, the government effectively split into two parts, each with its own goals and policies.

The permanent division of the Empire, coupled with the ongoing invasions and decline of the army, in a very real sense signed the Empire's death warrant. The first series of crises following the 395 split grew out of the new political situation that existed in the wake of Theodosius's death. The delegation of power to Honorius and Arcadius disturbed the Visigoths. In their minds, the deal they had made with Theodosius shortly after the Battle of Adrianople might only be valid while he personally sat on the throne. Now that he was gone and his sons ruled separate sections of the realm, the Visigoths might lose their federate status and perhaps suffer in other ways.

Alaric Invades Italy

To maintain their security, therefore, the various Visigothic bands came together under one ruler—Alaric. He tried to renegotiate the treaty of 382 and also demanded that the central government give him command of a Roman army. The government turned him down. So he led his warriors on a rampage through Thrace. Over the course of the next few years, Alaric continued making demands, while the disunity and weakness of the young emperors and their advisers played into his hands. In about 402 the Visigothic army marched on Italy. It was stopped by a Roman force led by the western ruler Honorius's tough and talented barbarian general Stilicho.

In the long run, however, Alaric's forward momentum was only temporarily slowed, and the threat he and his army posed had a ripple effect that further weakened the western Empire. When Italy was threatened by the oncoming Visigoths, Honorius felt he had no choice but to recall most of the soldiers stationed in Britain. This unwise move left that province largely unguarded; and various tribes, including the Picts and Saxons, launched raids on British towns and farms. A few years later, these invaders overran the island, and Rome lost one of its most important provinces.

At the same time, other restless and ambitious tribes were inspired by Alaric's boldness. In 406 armies of Vandals, Alani, and Suevi invaded Gaul. Some forged onward into Rome's Spanish provinces, and, because Honorius's government lacked the money and men to stop them, the in-truders were able to settle permanently in the conquered regions.

These Roman setbacks filled Alaric with new boldness and ambition. In 408 he regrouped his forces and marched on Italy again, this time reaching Rome with little or no opposition. Alaric was well aware that Rome was no longer the im-perial capital, which was now located at Ravenna, in northeastern Italy; but he also knew that Rome was still the Em-

This eighteenth-century engraving of Rome being destroyed by Alaric's army in 410 is entirely fanciful. In fact, the Visigoths stole gold, jewels, and other valuables, but left the city intact.

pire's largest city and the chief symbol of more than a thousand years of Roman power and prestige. Rather than risk seeing the great city captured by a foreign enemy, he reasoned, Honorius would surely meet his demands. And so, University College scholar Peter Heather explains:

> Alaric sat outside Rome and threatened to sack it unless the imperial authorities in Ravenna negotiated with him. His demands at this point were . . . [the offer of] a military alliance with the Roman state, demanding, in return, a generalship for himself, a large annual payment of gold, substantial corn supplies, and his troops to be settled in [nearby Roman provinces]. Such a position would have allowed the Goths to control Ravenna and routes over the Alps. . . . These demands were rejected. . . . Honorius, the western emperor, was willing to sacrifice Rome rather than negotiate.[81]

Angry over the government's refusal to deal with him, Alaric sacked Rome on August 24, 410. His men stayed only a few days and did little physical damage to the many stately public buildings. The real and more lasting injury was psychological in nature, for it was the first time that "invincible" Rome had been entered by a foreign foe in eight hundred years, and the event sent shock waves through the whole Mediterranean world. In faraway Palestine, the now-famous Christian writer Jerome remarked, "My voice is stopped, and sobs cut off the words as I try to speak. Captive is the city which once took captive all the world."[82]

"Last of the Romans"

Rome was not actually "captive," since Alaric pulled his troops out and soon afterward died; his successor, Athaulf, then led the Visigoths out of Italy and into southern Gaul. However, Jerome's emotional cry of dismay might well have been applied to the western Empire as a whole, for little by little, piece by piece, it was being captured and absorbed by barbarian tribes. For the remainder of his reign, Honorius tried to stem the continuing onslaught of invaders and settlers, but he was largely unsuccessful. He simply lacked the money, manpower, and military skill and ingenuity to mount a counteroffensive on the huge scale that was needed.

After Honorius died in 423, for a brief period a strong Roman military figure—Aëtius—emerged, and there seemed at least some hope that Rome's declining fortunes might be reversed. Aëtius, who later became known as "the last of the Romans," came to power in the following manner. The eastern emperor, Theodosius II, who had succeeded Arcadius on his death in 408, wanted to have a say in choosing Honorius's replacement. So Theodosius sent troops to Ravenna to make sure that Honorius's six-year-old nephew, Valentinian III, was installed on the throne. Since the boy was obviously too young to rule on his own, his mother,

Aided by the Visigoths and Burgundians, the Roman general Aëtius defeats Attila and his Huns at Chalons in 451.

Galla Placidia, assumed most of his duties. To her credit, she was a strong, capable ruler who for nearly ten years managed to administer what was left of the realm while keeping the ambitious military generals at bay. In the early 430s, however, Aëtius gained enough influence over the army and the maturing Valentinian to supercede Galla's authority. Although he was never emperor, for the next two decades Aëtius was the dominant figure in the western Roman sphere.

While a young man, Aëtius had been held hostage by the Huns and had come to know and trust certain Hunnic leaders. Now, as Rome's supreme military leader, he marshaled many Hunnic soldiers to fill out the dwindling ranks of the Roman army. (In the long run, this proved a destructive policy, since it further "barbarized" the army. In Aëtius's day, Roman citizens born in Italy and the remaining provinces made up only a small percentage of the troops.) A tough, stubborn, and skilled fighter, and apparently a Roman patriot in his own way, Aëtius led his forces in numerous campaigns designed to break the power of the various barbarian groups occupying Gaul. He defeated both the Visigoths and Burgundians, the latter quite decisively. And had his momentum continued, he might have gone on to bring Spain and perhaps even Britain back into the Roman fold.

However, events in eastern Europe steadily conspired to derail Aëtius's efforts. In the early 440s, a new and par-

ticularly savage Hunnic war leader named Attila emerged and gained the allegiance of most of the Huns. Living up to his nickname, the "Scourge of God," Attila attacked some of the eastern Roman provinces and eventually marched on Gaul. Most of Aëtius's Hunnic troops joined the approaching marauder, leaving him no choice but to make an alliance with his former enemies, the Visigoths and Burgundians. This combined force of Romans and barbarians narrowly defeated Attila at Chalons (or

Attila invades Italy. Bishop Leo I convinced him to withdraw, and the Hunnic leader died unexpectedly soon afterwards.

the Catalaunian Plains), in northeastern Gaul, in 451.

But now, at the height of his success, Aëtius made what amounted to a fatal error. Probably fearing to upset the balance of power among the northern tribes and thereby cause more invasions, he did not chase down and destroy Attila once and for all. This allowed Attila to regroup his forces, and soon he marched on Italy. Only the intervention of Leo I, bishop of Rome, and Attila's sudden death soon afterward stopped the Huns from sacking the former capital. Fortunately for Rome, the Hunnic forces swiftly dissipated, never to rise again. However, as Charles Freeman phrases it:

> The strategy of Aetius was now thoroughly discredited. He had not even been able to defend Italy. His enemies now saw their opportunity. Aetius was summoned to the emperor's presence in Ravenna and executed, possibly by Valentinian himself. Six months later, some officers loyal to Aetius had their revenge and struck down Valentinian.[83]

Rome's Last Transformation

In the wake of Aëtius's demise, no strong leader committed to maintaining the Empire's integrity emerged to replace him. The last nine western emperors were all weak rulers who lacked the talent and resources to protect the remaining Roman heartland, which was increasingly vulnerable to attack by barbarian forces. Valentinian's immediate successor, Petronius Maximus, who came to power in March 455, lasted only eleven weeks. He was killed fleeing from the Vandals, who sacked Rome in June. In prior years they had crossed from Spain into Africa, overrun Rome's fertile North African provinces, and gained federate status. Now, led by a king named Gaiseric, they sailed north and looted Rome for two weeks, kidnapping Valentinian's widow and two daughters in the process. Three years later, Gaiseric further crippled and humiliated the Empire by capturing Sicily, which had been a cherished Roman possession for almost seven centuries.

In fact, there was increasingly little left in the western realm that could be called Roman in the traditional sense. The western Empire now consisted of little more than the Italian peninsula and portions of a few nearby provinces. Moreover, most of the soldiers still defending these lands, including the generals, were of barbarian birth and had little understanding of or concern for the old Roman ideals and traditions. The military strongman who dominated the West from about 456 to 472, for example, was half Visigoth and half Sueve. Called Ricimer, he used his military muscle to choose and depose a series of ineffectual puppet emperors, including Majorian (reigned 457–461), Libius Severus (461–465), Anthemius (467–472), and Olybrius (472).

Alarmed at the political corruption and chaos in Italy, the eastern emperor,

The Vandals sack Rome in 455. The city suffered physical devastation, although most of the damage was soon repaired.

Zeno, tried to intervene and restore order, an attempt that proved much too little and too late. In 474 he sent nobleman Julius Nepos to take the western throne. However, Nepos was overthrown by his leading general, Orestes, who made his own son, Romulus Augustulus, emperor.

All this political intriguing and gamesmanship proved futile. The naked truth was that none of these men held any real power, which actually lay in the hands of the German mercenaries who by now controlled the last of Rome's armies. On September 4, 476, the leading German-born general, Flavius Odoacer, led a contingent of troops into Ravenna. He demanded that Romulus Augustulus step down, and the young man, having no choice, did so and quietly retired to Naples.

Odoacer became king of Italy, and no more puppet rulers were placed on the Roman throne by him or his successors. Therefore, historians came to mark Romulus Augustulus's forced abdication as the end of the traditional western imperial government and the "fall of Rome." This can be misleading, as Rome still stood and its people went about their business as usual, despite the fact that their rulers were now Germans.

In general, and to their credit, these new rulers tried to maintain an ordered society and showed considerable respect for most Roman traditions and institutions. But their efforts came to nothing in the end. The former Roman Empire had been reduced to a patchwork quilt of

The German-born general Odoacer (right) forces the boy-emperor Romulus Augustulus to step down from the throne. This marked the official end of Rome's imperial government.

Was Julius Nepos Actually the Last Emperor?

Historian Michael Grant makes the case here (from his book The Visible Past*) that Julius Nepos, Romulus Augustulus's immediate predecessor, might actually have been the last official Roman emperor.*

Nepos had married into the family of the eastern emperor Leo I, who helped him to secure the western throne. . . . His succession was confirmed by the Roman Senate and by some measure, at least, of popular support. . . . Nepos gave his principal military post, the Mastership of Soldiers at the Ravenna headquarters, to Orestes, formerly secretary to Attila the Hun. But when Nepos lost Gaul [to the Goths] . . . Orestes decided to replace him on the western throne by his own son Romulus "Augustulus." With this aim, Orestes led a force to attack Ravenna, whereupon Nepos . . . made his escape by sea and withdrew to his princedom of Dalmatia [on the western edge of the Adriatic Sea]. [Not long after Odoacer had deposed Romulus Augustulus in 476,] the eastern emperor, now Leo's son-in-law Zeno, received two ambassadors. One was from Odoacer, who urged formal recognition for himself in the West. . . . The other . . . came from Nepos in Dalmatia, who reminded Zeno of their marriage connection . . . and appealed for support to regain the western throne. . . . Although Odoacer . . . took no steps to invite Nepos back to Italy, he accorded him the recognition that the eastern emperor had requested. . . . [Nepos] was assassinated [in 480] by two members of his staff in his country house. . . . The last Roman emperor of any part of the West had now ceased to rule.

barbarian kingdoms interspersed among stretches of disputed, lawless territories. In the next two centuries, the old Roman world would undergo the last of its great transformations. The surviving kingdoms of those who had overrun Rome would become medieval realms, which would absorb Christianity and other aspects of old Roman culture and with these tools create a new European world.

Notes

Introduction: What the Histories Do Not Tell

1. Thomas Wiedemann, *Greek and Roman Slavery*. London: Croom Helm, 1981, p. 100.
2. Robert B. Kebric, *Roman People*. Mountain View, CA: Mayfield, 2001, p. 2.
3. Jo-Ann Shelton, ed., *As the Romans Did: A Sourcebook in Roman Social History*. New York: Oxford University Press, 1988, pp. viii–ix.
4. L.P. Wilkinson, *The Roman Experience*. Lanham, MD: University Press of America, 1974, p. 5.

Chapter 1: Rome's Origins and Early Rulers

5. Livy, *The History of Rome from Its Foundation*, books 1–5 published as *Livy: The Early History of Rome*, trans. Aubrey de Sélincourt. New York: Penguin, 1960, p. 38.
6. Livy, *Early History of Rome*, pp. 39, 40.
7. T.J. Cornell, *The Beginnings of Rome: Italy and Rome from the Bronze Age to the Punic Wars (c. 1000–264 B.C.)*. London: Routledge, 1995, pp. 48, 54–55.
8. Cornell, *Beginnings of Rome*, p. 65.
9. Virgil, *The Aeneid*, trans. Patric Dickinson. New York: New American Library, 1961, pp. 141–42.
10. Virgil, *Aeneid*, p. 14.
11. Plutarch, *Life of Romulus*, in *Parallel Lives*, published complete as *Lives of the Noble Grecians and Romans*, trans. John Dryden. New York: Random House, 1932, p. 31.
12. Livy, *Early History of Rome*, pp. 42–43.
13. Livy, *Early History of Rome*, pp. 43–45.
14. Michael Rostovtzeff, *Rome*, trans. J.D. Duff. London: Oxford University Press, 1960, pp. 19–20.
15. Livy, *Early History of Rome*, p. 81.
16. Livy, *Early History of Rome*, p. 83.
17. Livy, *Early History of Rome*, p. 61.
18. Livy, *Early History of Rome*, p. 61.

Chapter 2: Founding and Expansion of the Republic

19. Charles Freeman, *Egypt, Greece, and Rome: Civilizations of the Ancient Mediterranean*. Oxford: Oxford University Press, 1996, pp. 314–15.
20. Cornell, *Beginnings of Rome*, p. 217.
21. Livy, *Early History of Rome*, p. 99.
22. Livy, *Early History of Rome*, pp. 115–17.
23. Cicero, *Laws*, in *Cicero: On Government*, trans. Michael Grant. New York: Penguin, 1993, p. 196.
24. Michael Grant, *History of Rome*. New York: Scribner's, 1978, pp. 70–71.
25. Cicero, *For Cluentius*, in *Cicero: Murder Trials*, trans. Michael Grant. New York: Penguin, 1990, pp. 216–17.

26. Quoted in Plutarch, *Life of Pyrrhus,* in *The Age of Alexander: Nine Greek Lives by Plutarch,* trans. Ian Scott-Kilvert. New York: Penguin, 1973, p. 409.

27. Quoted in Plutarch, *Life of Pyrrhus,* in *Age of Alexander,* p. 412.

28. Livy, *The History of Rome from Its Foundation,* books 21–30 published as *Livy: The War with Hannibal,* trans. Aubrey de Sélincourt. New York: Penguin, 1972, pp. 154–55.

29. Quoted in Polybius, *The Histories,* published as *Polybius: The Rise of the Roman Empire,* trans. Ian Scott-Kilvert. New York: Penguin, 1979, pp. 299–300.

Chapter 3: Fall of the Republic and Rise of the Empire

30. Appian, *Roman History,* excerpted in *Appian: The Civil Wars,* trans. John Carter. New York: Penguin, 1996, pp. 287–88.

31. Ronald Syme, *The Roman Revolution.* New York: Oxford University Press, 1960, p. 15.

32. Plutarch, *Life of Sulla,* in *Fall of the Roman Republic: Six Lives by Plutarch,* trans. Rex Warner. New York: Penguin, 1972, pp. 104–105.

33. Plutarch, *Life of Crassus,* in *Fall of the Roman Republic,* p. 120.

34. Plutarch, *Life of Crassus,* in *Fall of the Roman Republic,* p. 126.

35. Plutarch, *Life of Cicero,* in *Fall of the Roman Republic,* pp. 332–33.

36. Plutarch, *Life of Caesar,* in *Fall of the Roman Republic,* p. 257.

37. Plutarch, *Life of Caesar,* in *Fall of the Roman Republic,* p. 259.

38. Quoted in Suetonius, *Julius Caesar,* in *Lives of the Twelve Caesars,* published as *The Twelve Caesars,* trans. Robert Graves, rev. Michael Grant. New York: Penguin, 1979, p. 28.

39. Plutarch, *Life of Antony,* in *Makers of Rome: Nine Lives by Plutarch,* trans. Ian Scott-Kilvert. New York: Penguin, 1965, p. 283.

40. Appian, *Roman History,* trans. Horace White. Cambridge: Harvard University Press, 1964, p. 106.

41. Dio Cassius, *Roman History: The Reign of Augustus,* trans. Ian Scott-Kilvert. New York: Penguin, 1987, p. 123.

42. Quoted in Dio Cassius, *Roman History,* p. 140.

Chapter 4: The Pax Romana: Rome at Its Zenith

43. Livy, *Early History of Rome,* p. 402.

44. Suetonius, *Augustus,* in *The Twelve Caesars,* pp. 69–70.

45. Suetonius, *Augustus,* in *The Twelve Caesars,* p. 103.

46. Suetonius, *Augustus,* in *The Twelve Caesars,* pp. 110, 111.

47. Tacitus, *Annals,* published as *Tacitus: The Annals of Imperial Rome,* trans. Michael Grant. New York: Penguin, 1989, pp. 37–38.

48. Quoted in Suetonius, *Caligula,* in *The Twelve Caesars,* pp. 168, 170.

49. Suetonius, *Nero,* in *The Twelve Caesars,* pp. 227–228.

50. Suetonius, *Nero,* in *The Twelve Caesars,* pp. 239–40.

51. Suetonius, *Nero,* in *The Twelve Caesars,* p. 243.

52. Chris Scarre, *Chronicle of the Roman Emperors.* New York: Thames and Hudson, 1995, p. 46.

53. Suetonius, *Claudius,* in *The Twelve Caesars,* p. 201.

54. Suetonius, *Vespasian,* in *The Twelve Caesars,* p. 285.

55. Suetonius, *Titus,* in *The Twelve Caesars,* pp. 295–96.

56. Suetonius, *Titus,* in *The Twelve Caesars,* p. 296.

57. Edward Gibbon, *The Decline and Fall of the Roman Empire,* ed. David Womersley. 3 vols. New York: Penguin, 1994, vol. 1, pp. 101–103.

58. Pliny the Younger, *Panegyric Addressed to the Emperor Trajan,* excerpted in Naphtali Lewis and Meyer Reinhold, eds., *Roman Civilization, Sourcebook II: The Empire.* New York: Harper and Row, 1966, p. 100.

59. Aelius Aristides, *Roman Panegyric,* excerpted in Lewis and Reinhold, *Sourcebook II: The Empire,* pp. 100, 137–38.

60. Michael Grant, *The Roman Emperors.* New York: Barnes and Noble, 1997, p. 87.

Chapter 5: Near Collapse and Rebirth: The Later Empire

61. Other common names for this chaotic period include "the century of crisis," "the crisis of the third century," "the military monarchy," and "the age of the soldier-emperors."

62. Anthony Kamm, *The Romans: An Introduction.* London: Routledge, 1995, p. 185.

63. Quoted in Dio Cassius, *Roman History,* quoted in Scarre, *Chronicle of the Roman Emperors,* p. 138.

64. Scarre, *Chronicle of the Roman Emperors,* p. 146.

65. Herodian, *History,* quoted in Lewis and Reinhold, *Sourcebook II: The Empire,* pp. 437–38.

66. Michael Grant, *The Fall of the Roman Empire.* New York: Macmillan, 1990, p. 3.

67. Arthur E.R. Boak and William G. Sinnigen, *A History of Rome to 565 A.D.* New York: Macmillan, 1965, p. 429.

68. *Life of Carus,* in *Augustan History,* published as *Lives of the Later Caesars, the First Part of the Augustan History, with Newly Compiled Lives of Nerva and Trajan,* trans. Anthony Birley. New York: Penguin, 1976, p. 32.

69. Diocletian, *Economic Edict,* in Lewis and Reinhold, *Sourcebook II: The Empire,* p. 465.

70. Eusebius, *Life of Constantine,* quoted in Stewart Perowne, *Caesars and Saints: The Rise of the Christian State, A.D. 180–313.* 1962. Reprint, New York: Barnes and Noble, 1992, p. 175.

71. Actually, although the two men agreed on the basic provisions of the edict, they did not publish it while in Milan. Licinius was unexpectedly called away from the conference and issued the decree a few months later in both their names.

72. *Edict of Milan,* in Eusebius, *Ecclesiastical History,* trans. Roy J. Deferrari. 2 vols. Washington, D.C.: Catholic University of America Press, 1955, vol. 1, p. 269.

73. Kebric, *Roman People,* p. 274.

Chapter 6: Rome's Decline and Disintegration

74. Grant, *Fall of the Roman Empire,* p. xi.

75. Gibbon, *Decline and Fall,* vol. 2, p. 512.

76. Grant, *Fall of the Roman Empire,* p. xii.

77. Gibbon, *Decline and Fall,* vol. 2, p. 512.
78. Ammianus Marcellinus, *History,* published as *The Later Roman Empire, A.D. 354–378,* trans. and ed. Walter Hamilton. New York: Penguin, 1986, pp. 411–12.
79. Ammianus, *History,* p. 435.
80. Arther Ferrill, *The Fall of the Roman Empire: The Military Explanation.* New York: Thames and Hudson, 1986, pp. 84–85, 140.
81. Peter Heather, *The Goths.* Cambridge, MA: Blackwell, 1996, p. 148.
82. Jerome, *Letter 127,* in Leon Bernard and Theodore B. Hodges, eds., *Readings in European History.* New York: Macmillan, 1958, p. 44.
83. Freeman, *Egypt, Greece, and Rome,* p. 523.

Chronology

B.C.

ca. 1000
Latin tribesmen establish small villages on some of the Seven Hills marking the site of the future city of Rome.

753
Traditional founding date for the city of Rome by Romulus (as computed and accepted by Roman scholars some seven centuries later).

509
The leading Roman landowners throw out their last king and establish the Roman Republic.

ca. 451–450
The Twelve Tables, Rome's first law code, are inscribed and set up.

340–338
Rome defeats the Latin League, an alliance of Italian city-states, and incorporates the territories of some of its members into the growing Roman state.

312
The building of Rome's first major road, the Appian Way, and its first aqueduct, the Aqua Appia, begins.

280–275
The Romans fight several battles with the Greek Hellenistic king Pyrrhus, who has come to the aid of the Greek cities of southern Italy; his victories are so costly that he abandons the Italian Greeks to their fate.

265
Having gained control of the Italian Greek cities, Rome is master of the whole Italian peninsula.

264–241
Years of the First Punic War, in which Rome defeats the maritime empire of Carthage.

218–201
Rome fights Carthage again in the Second Punic War, in which the Carthaginian general Hannibal crosses the Alps, invades Italy, and delivers the Romans one crippling defeat after another.

200–197
The Romans defeat Macedonia in the Second Macedonian War.

149–146
Rome annihilates Carthage in the Third Punic War.

100
Birth of Julius Caesar, one of the greatest statesmen and military generals in history.

ca. 80
The first all-stone Roman amphitheater opens in the town of Pompeii.

73–71
The Thracian slave Spartacus leads the last of Rome's large slave rebellions; the Roman nobleman Marcus Crassus eventually defeats the slaves.

65
Caesar stages the first large public gladiatorial combats in Rome.

58–51

Caesar conquers the peoples of Transalpine Gaul.

49

Caesar crosses the Rubicon River, initiating a civil war; the following year he defeats his chief rival, Pompey, at Pharsalus (in Greece).

44

After declaring himself "dictator for life," Caesar is assassinated by a group of senators.

42

Roman strongmen Mark Antony and Octavian (Caesar's adopted son) defeat the leaders of the conspiracy against Caesar at Philippi (in northern Greece). At this point, the Republic is effectively dead.

31

Octavian defeats Antony and Egypt's Queen Cleopatra at Actium (in western Greece) and gains firm control of the Mediterranean world. Soon the Senate confers on him the title of Augustus, "the revered one," and he becomes, in effect, Rome's first emperor.

ca. 30 B.C.–A.D. 180

The approximate years of the so-called Pax Romana ("Roman Peace"), a period in which the Mediterranean world under the first several Roman emperors enjoys relative peace and prosperity.

20

Augustus sets up a board of curators to manage Italy's public highways.

4

Jesus is born in Bethlehem (in the Roman province of Judaea).

A.D.

6

Augustus establishes a firefighting force (the *vigiles*) to protect the Roman capital.

14

Augustus dies, plunging the Roman people into a period of deep mourning; he is succeeded by Tiberius.

ca. 30–33

Jesus is executed on the orders of Pontius Pilate, the Roman governor of Judaea.

64

A great fire ravages large sections of Rome; the emperor Nero unfairly blames the disaster on the Christians and initiates the first of a series of persecutions against them.

79

The volcano Mount Vesuvius erupts, burying the Italian towns of Pompeii and Herculaneum; the great naturalist Pliny the Elder dies while observing the disaster up close.

80

The emperor Titus inaugurates the Colosseum, Rome's greatest amphitheater.

98–117

Reign of the emperor Trajan, in which the Roman Empire reaches its greatest size and power.

ca. 122

The emperor Hadrian visits Britain and plans the construction of the massive defensive wall that will bear his name.

180

Death of the emperor Marcus Aurelius, marking the end of the Pax Romana era and beginning of Rome's steady slide into economic and political crisis.

212

The emperor Caracalla extends citizenship rights to all free adult males in the Empire.

235–284

The Empire suffers under the strain of terrible political upheaval and civil strife, prompting later historians to call this period the Anarchy.

284

Diocletian ascends the throne and initiates sweeping political, economic, and social reforms, in effect reconstructing the Empire under a new blueprint. (Modern historians often call this new realm the Later Empire.)

306–337

Reign of the emperor Constantine I, who carries on the reforms begun by Diocletian.

313

Constantine and his eastern colleague, Licinius, issue the so-called Edict of Milan, granting religious toleration to the formerly hated and persecuted Christians.

330

Constantine founds the city of Constantinople, on the Bosphorus Strait, making it the capital of the eastern section of the Empire.

337

Constantine dies; he converts to Christianity on his deathbed.

ca. 370

The Huns, a savage nomadic people from central Asia, sweep into eastern Europe, pushing the Goths and other "barbarian" peoples into the northern Roman provinces.

378

The eastern emperor Valens is disastrously defeated by the Visigoths at Adrianople (in northern Greece).

391

At the urgings of Christian leaders, especially the bishop Ambrose, the emperor Theodosius I closes the pagan temples, demolishing some and turning others into museums. In less than a century, Christianity has become the Empire's official religion.

395

The last emperor to rule both western and eastern Rome, Theodosius, dies and leaves his young sons, Honorius and Arcadius, in charge of a divided realm.

ca. 407

As Rome steadily loses control of several of its northern and western provinces, Britain falls under the sway of barbarian tribes.

410

Alaric, king of the Visigoths, briefly occupies and loots Rome.

451

Aëtius, often called "the last of the Romans," defeats Attila the Hun at Chalons, in Gaul. Soon afterward, Aëtius dies at the hands of the emperor Valentinian III.

455

The Vandals sack Rome.

476

The German-born general Odoacer demands that the emperor, the young Romulus Augustulus, grant him and his men federate status; when the emperor refuses, Odoacer deposes him and no new emperor takes his place. The succession of Roman emperors continues in the eastern realm, which steadily evolves into the Byzantine Empire.

For Further Reading

Isaac Asimov, *The Roman Empire*. Boston: Houghton Mifflin, 1967. An excellent overview of the main events of the Empire; so precise and clearly written that even very basic readers will benefit.

Lionel Casson, *Daily Life in Ancient Rome*. New York: American Heritage, 1975. A well-written presentation by a highly respected scholar of how the Romans lived: their homes, streets, entertainments, eating habits, theaters, religion, slaves, marriage customs, tombstone epitaphs, and more.

Phil R. Cox and Annabel Spenceley, *Who Were the Romans?* New York: EDC Publications, 1994. An impressive, well-illustrated introduction to the Romans, presented in a question-and-answer format and aimed at basic readers.

Susie Hodge, *Roman Art*. Crystal Lake, IL: Heineman Library, 1998. A short but well-illustrated and informative look at ancient Roman art and sculpture.

John Malam, *Secret Worlds: Gladiators*. London: Dorling Kindersley, 2002. A beautifully illustrated book that brings the exciting but bloody gladiatorial combats of ancient Rome to life.

Geraldine McCaughrean, *Roman Myths*. New York: Macmillan, 2001. An extremely well-written introduction to Roman mythology for young people. The author's prose is enthusiastic and readable.

Don Nardo, *The Age of Augustus*. San Diego: Lucent Books, 1996. An overview of the reign and accomplishments of the man who created the Roman Empire and oversaw the golden age of Roman literature.

———, *Roman Amphitheaters*. New York: Franklin Watts, 2002. Tells about the origins of the stone arenas where gladiators and animal hunters fought and often died, how these structures were built, and the variety of games they showcased.

Jonathan Rutland, *See Inside a Roman Town*. New York: Barnes and Noble, 1986. A very attractively illustrated introduction to major concepts of Roman civilization for basic readers.

Judith Simpson, *Ancient Rome*. New York: Time-Life Books, 1997. One of Time-Life's library of picture books about the ancient world, this one is beautifully illustrated with attractive and appropriate photographs and paintings. The general but well-written text is aimed at intermediate readers.

Chester G. Starr, *The Ancient Romans*. New York: Oxford University Press, 1971. A clearly written survey of Roman history, featuring several interesting sidebars on such subjects as the Etruscans, Roman law, and the Roman army. Also contains many primary source quotes by Roman and Greek writers. For intermediate and advanced younger readers.

Major Works Consulted

Ancient Sources

Paul J. Alexander, ed., *The Ancient World: To 300 A.D.* New York: Macmillan, 1963.

Ammianus Marcellinus, *History,* published as *The Later Roman Empire, A.D. 354–378.* Trans. and Ed. Walter Hamilton. New York: Penguin, 1986.

Appian, *Roman History.* Trans. Horace White. Cambridge: Harvard University Press, 1964; and excerpted in *Appian: The Civil Wars.* Trans. John Carter. New York: Penguin, 1996.

Augustan History, published as *Lives of the Later Caesars, the First Part of the* Augustan History, *with Newly Compiled Lives of Nerva and Trajan.* Trans. Anthony Birley. New York: Penguin, 1976.

Leon Bernard and Theodore B. Hodges, eds., *Readings in European History.* New York: Macmillan, 1958.

Cicero, *De Officiis (On Duties).* Trans. Walter Miller. Cambridge: Harvard University Press, 1961; *Selected Political Speeches of Cicero.* Trans. Michael Grant. Baltimore: Penguin, 1979; *Cicero: Murder Trials.* Trans. Michael Grant. New York: Penguin, 1990; and *Cicero: On Government.* Trans. Michael Grant. New York: Penguin, 1993.

Dio Cassius, *Roman History: The Reign of Augustus.* Trans. Ian Scott-Kilvert. New York: Penguin, 1987.

Eusebius, *Ecclesiastical History.* Trans. Roy J. Deferrari. 2 vols. Washington, D.C.: Catholic University of America Press, 1955.

Naphtali Lewis and Meyer Reinhold, eds., *Roman Civilization, Sourcebook I: The Republic,* and *Roman Civilization, Sourcebook II: The Empire.* New York: Harper and Row, 1966.

Livy, *The History of Rome from Its Foundation,* books 1–5 published as *Livy: The Early History of Rome.* Trans. Aubrey de Sélincourt. New York: Penguin, 1960; books 21–30 published as *Livy: The War with Hannibal.* Trans. Aubrey de Sélincourt. New York: Penguin, 1972; books 31–45 published as *Livy: Rome and the Mediterranean.* Trans. Henry Bettenson. New York: Penguin, 1976. Also, various books excerpted in *Livy,* vol. 2, Trans. Canon Roberts. New York: E.P. Dutton, 1912.

Marcus Aurelius, *Meditations.* Trans. George Long, in *Great Books of the Western World,* vol. 12, Chicago: Encyclopedia Britannica, 1952.

Pliny the Elder, *Natural History.* Trans. H. Rackham. 10 vols. Cambridge: Harvard University Press, 1967; and excerpted in *Pliny the Elder: Natural History: A Selection.* Trans. John H. Healy. New York: Penguin, 1991.

Pliny the Younger, *Letters.* Trans. William Melmouth. 2 vols. Cambridge: Harvard University Press, 1961; also translated by Betty Radice in *The Letters of the Younger Pliny.* New York: Penguin, 1969.

Plutarch, *Parallel Lives,* published complete as *Lives of the Noble Grecians and Romans.* Trans. John Dryden. New York: Random House, 1932; also excerpted in *The Age of Alexander: Nine Greek Lives by Plutarch.* Trans. Ian Scott-Kilvert. New York: Penguin, 1973; *Fall of the Roman Republic: Six Lives by Plutarch.* Trans. Rex Warner. New York: Penguin, 1972; and *Makers of Rome: Nine Lives by Plutarch.* Trans. Ian Scott-Kilvert. New York: Penguin, 1965.

Polybius, *The Histories,* published as *Polybius: The Rise of the Roman Empire.* Trans. Ian Scott-Kilvert. New York: Penguin, 1979.

Jo-Ann Shelton, ed., *As the Romans Did: A Sourcebook in Roman Social History.* New York: Oxford University Press, 1988.

William G. Sinnegin, ed., *Sources in Western Civilization: Rome.* New York: Free Press, 1965.

Suetonius, *Lives of the Twelve Caesars,* published as *The Twelve Caesars.* Trans. Robert Graves, rev. Michael Grant. New York: Penguin, 1979.

Tacitus, *Annals,* published as *Tacitus: The Annals of Imperial Rome.* Trans. Michael Grant. New York: Penguin, 1989.

Virgil, *The Aeneid.* Trans. Patric Dickinson. New York: New American Library, 1961; also *Works.* Trans. H. Rushton Fairclough. 2 vols. Cambridge: Harvard University Press, 1967.

Modern Sources

Averil Cameron, *The Later Roman Empire: A.D. 284–430.* Cambridge: Harvard University Press, 1993. This well-written, somewhat scholarly volume contains excellent general up-to-date summaries of Diocletian's administrative and other reforms and Constantine's own reforms, including his acceptance of Christianity.

Peter Connolly, *Greece and Rome at War.* London: Macdonald, 1981. A highly informative and useful volume by one of the finest historians of ancient military affairs. Connolly, whose stunning paintings adorn this and his other books, is also the foremost modern illustrator of the ancient world. Highly recommended.

T.J. Cornell, *The Beginnings of Rome: Italy and Rome from the Bronze Age to the Punic Wars (c. 1000–264 B.C.).* London: Routledge, 1995. This well-written, authoritative study of Rome's early centuries offers compelling arguments for rejecting certain long-held notions about these years, especially the idea that the Etruscans took over and ruled Rome. Very highly recommended.

F.R. Cowell, *Cicero and the Roman Republic.* Baltimore: Penguin, 1967. A very detailed and insightful analysis of the late Republic, its leaders, and the problems that led to its collapse. Highly recommended.

Michael Crawford, *The Roman Republic.* Cambridge: Harvard University Press, 1993. This is one of the best available overviews of the Republic, offering various insights into the nature of the political, cultural, and intellectual forces that shaped the decisions of Roman leaders.

Arther Ferrill, *The Fall of the Roman Empire: The Military Explanation.* New York: Thames and Hudson, 1986. In this excellent work, written in a straightforward style, Ferrill builds a strong case for the idea that Rome fell mainly because its army grew increasingly less disciplined and formidable in the Empire's last two centuries, while at the same time the overall defensive strategy of the emperors was ill-conceived and contributed to the ultimate fall.

John B. Firth, *Augustus Caesar and the Organization of the Empire of Rome.* Freeport, NY: Books for the Libraries Press, 1972. Beginning with Caesar's assassination in 44 B.C., this is a detailed, thoughtful telling of the final years of the Republic, including Octavian's rise to power during the civil wars and his ascendancy as Augustus, the first Roman emperor.

Michael Grant, *Caesar.* London: Weidenfeld and Nicolson, 1974. A fine telling of Caesar's exploits and importance by one of the most prolific of classical historians.

———, *Constantine the Great: The Man and His Times.* New York: Scribner's, 1994. An excellent study of Constantine, his achievements (Christianity, Constantinople, etc.), and his impact on the Roman Empire and later ages.

———, *The Fall of the Roman Empire.* New York: Macmillan, 1990. Grant begins here with a general historical sketch of Rome's last centuries, and then proceeds with his main thesis, that Rome fell because of many manifestations of disunity, among them generals turning on the state, the poor versus the rich, the bureaucrats versus the people, the pagans versus the Christians, and so forth. An excellent resource filled with useful facts and interesting theories.

———, *History of Rome.* New York: Scribner's, 1978. Comprehensive, insightful, and well written, this is one of the best available general overviews of Roman civilization from its founding to its fall.

A.H.M. Jones, *Constantine and the Conversion of Europe.* Toronto: University of Toronto Press, 1978. A superior general overview of Constantine's world and his influence, particularly in the area of religion, by one of the twentieth century's greatest Roman scholars.

———, *The Decline of the Ancient World.* London: Longman Group, 1966. Note: This is a shortened version of Jones's massive and highly influential *The Later Roman Empire,* 284–602. 3 vols. 1964. Reprint, Norman: University of Oklahoma Press, 1975. An exhaustively detailed, endlessly informative work that touches on virtually every aspect of the history and culture of the Later Empire.

Chris Scarre, *Chronicle of the Roman Emperors.* New York: Thames and Hudson, 1995. A well-written general overview of the emperors, supplemented by numerous primary source materials and useful timelines.

Additional Works Consulted

Lesley Adkins and Roy A. Adkins, *Handbook to Life in Ancient Rome*. New York: Facts On File, 1994.

E. Badian, *Roman Imperialism in the Late Republic*. Ithaca, NY: Cornell University Press, 1968.

Paul G. Bahn, ed., *The Cambridge Illustrated History of Archaeology*. New York: Cambridge University Press, 1996.

R.H. Barrow, *The Romans*. Baltimore: Penguin, 1949.

Arthur E.R. Boak and William G. Sinnigen, *A History of Rome to 565 A.D.* New York: Macmillan, 1965.

Ernle Bradford, *Julius Caesar: The Pursuit of Power*. New York: Morrow, 1984.

Peter Brown, *The World of Late Antiquity, A.D. 150–750*. New York: Harcourt Brace, 1971.

Matthew Bunson, *A Dictionary of the Roman Empire*. Oxford: Oxford University Press, 1991.

Lionel Casson, *The Ancient Mariners*. New York: Macmillan, 1959.

———, *Travel in the Ancient World*. Baltimore: Johns Hopkins University Press, 1994.

Owen Chadwick, *A History of Christianity*. New York: St. Martin's Press, 1995.

Mortimer Chambers, ed., *The Fall of the Roman Empire: Can It Be Explained?* New York: Holt, Rinehart, and Winston, 1963.

Tim Cornell and John Matthews, *Atlas of the Roman World*. New York; Facts On File, 1982.

Donald R. Dudley, *The Civilization of Rome*. New York: New American Library, 1960.

———, *The Romans, 850 B.C.–A.D. 337.* New York: Knopf, 1970.

Charles Freeman, *Egypt, Greece, and Rome: Civilizations of the Ancient Mediterranean*. Oxford: Oxford University Press, 1996.

———, *The World of the Romans*. New York: Oxford University Press, 1993.

Jane F. Gardner, *Women in Roman Law and Society*. Indianapolis: Indiana University Press, 1986.

Edward Gibbon, *The Decline and Fall of the Roman Empire*. Ed. David Womersley. 3 vols. New York: Penguin, 1994.

Michael Grant, *The Ancient Mediterranean*. New York: Penguin, 1969.

———, *The Roman Emperors*. New York: Barnes and Noble, 1997.

———, *A Social History of Greece and Rome*. New York: Charles Scribner's Sons, 1992.

———, *The Visible Past: Recent Archaeological Discoveries of Greek and Roman History*. New York: Scribner's, 1990.

———, *The World of Rome*. New York: New American Library, 1960.

Peter Heather, *The Goths*. Cambridge, MA: Blackwell, 1996.

Anthony Kamm, *The Romans: An Introduction*. London: Routledge, 1995.

Robert B. Kebric, *Roman People*. Mountain View, CA: Mayfield, 2001.

Lawrence Keppie, *The Making of the Roman Army*. New York: Barnes and Noble, 1994.

Friedrich Munzer, *Roman Aristocratic Parties and Families*. Trans. Therese Ridley. Baltimore: Johns Hopkins University Press, 1999.

Stewart Perowne, *Caesars and Saints: The Rise of the Christian State, A.D. 180–313*. 1962. Reprints, New York: Barnes and Noble, 1992.

———, *The End of the Roman World*. New York: Thomas Y. Crowell, 1966.

Justine Davis Randers-Pehrson, *Barbarians and Romans: The Birth Struggle of Europe, A.D. 400–700*. Norman: University of Oklahoma Press, 1983.

Michael Rostovtzeff, *Rome*. Trans. J.D. Duff. London: Oxford University Press, 1960.

Henry T. Rowell, *Rome in the Augustan Age*. Norman: University of Oklahoma Press, 1962.

Chris Scarre, *Historical Atlas of Ancient Rome*. New York: Penguin, 1995.

Chester G. Starr, *Civilization and the Caesars: The Intellectual Revolution in the Roman Empire*. New York: Norton, 1965.

———, *A History of the Ancient World*. New York: Oxford University Press, 1991.

Ronald Syme, *The Roman Revolution*. New York: Oxford University Press, 1960.

Mortimer Wheeler, *Roman Art and Architecture*. New York: Praeger, 1964.

Thomas Wiedemann, *Greek and Roman Slavery*. London: Croom Helm, 1981.

L.P. Wilkinson, *The Roman Experience*. Lanham, MD: University Press of America, 1974.

Index

Picture Credits

About the Author

Classical historian Don Nardo has published many volumes about ancient
Roman history and culture, including *The Punic Wars, The Age of Augustus, A
Travel Guide to Ancient Rome, Life of a Roman Gladiator, Greek and Roman
Science,* and Greenhaven Press's massive *Encyclopedia of Greek and Roman
Mythology.* Mr. Nardo also writes screenplays and teleplays and composes
music. He lives in Massachusetts with his wife, Christine.